Glass Paperweights

JAMES MACKAY

Glass paperweights

WARD LOCK LIMITED
London

ISBN 0 7063 1102 7

First published in Great Britain 1973
by Ward Lock Limited, 116 Baker Street,
London, W1M 2BB

Designed by Denis Wrigley

Text phototypeset in 11/13pt Ehrhardt
by Filmtype Services Limited, Scarborough
Printed and bound by
Butler & Tanner Ltd., Frome and London

Page 1

A mushroom weight by
St Louis with coral and
white spirals round the
base. 3⅛ in.

Page 2

A dark-blue
overlay weight with 7
windows in blue and
white overlay with
traces of gilding. 3 in.

RIGHT Pompom
weight on a swirling
white latticinio
ground. 2¾ in.

Page 3

TOP A trefoil garland
on a coloured
ground. 3¼ in.

BOTTOM An unusual
pinchbeck weight with
a gilt-metal base
moulded in relief and
heightened with
coloured enamels.
3⅜ in.

Page 5

A primrose weight with
red, striped white
petals on a star-cut
base by Baccarat. 2⅝ in.

Acknowledgements

The author and publishers would like to thank the following for the
use of illustrative material in this book:
Christie, Manson & Wood, Philip Robinson, the Science
Museum, A. A. Shipton, Sotheby & Co., Alan Tillman Antiques,
the Victoria and Albert Museum and the Bergstrom Art Center
& Museum, Neenah, Wisconsin for permission to reproduce
material from *Glass Paperweights of the Bergstrom Art Center* by
Evelyn Campbell Cloak, Crown Publishers Inc., New York 1969.

A crown weight by St
Louis with red and
green, blue and lime
ribbons and white
spiral threads. 2⅝ in.

Contents

A butterfly and garland
weight on an upset-
muslin ground by
Baccarat. $2\frac{5}{8}$ in.

A double-clematis
weight with red petals
and an outer garland
on a star-cut base by
Baccarat. $2\frac{7}{8}$ in.

Upright bouquet
weight with concave
windows in the top and
sides. $3\frac{1}{4}$ in.

One

Their Origins

Although glass paperweights as we know them today date from the 1840s they can trace their ancestry back thousands of years. The ingredients of the paperweight – the tiny pieces of glass canes, rods and beads assembled into patterns and mosaics – were known to craftsmen working in Egypt about 1600 B.C., if not earlier. These elements were used to decorate tiles and vessels of all kinds. Intricate effects were created by trailing threads of molten glass of different colours over the predominant dark blue ground, and feathered or watered effects were created by scratching the molten glass with a sharp point. Some examples of glass-decorated wares from Egypt are known in which the threads of molten glass were twisted to give the *latticinio* effect which later became a popular motif in paperweights.

Dog-rose in clear glass with a star-cut base. 2¾ in.

The Egyptians also perfected the technique of making glass canes with a decorative motif seen in the cross-section. Layers of glass of different colours, or threads of coloured glass, were amalgamated, twisted and drawn out to form the rods and canes. In this way beads and other ornaments could be produced, the required amount being cut from a continuous length of cane. These multi-coloured canes provided the basic material, for *millefiori* decoration. This Italian term, meaning 'thousand flowers', describes the intricate arrangement of pieces of glass cane. Millefiori decoration was used in Egypt to ornament pottery vessels and plaques. The art of millefiori glass decoration continued to develop in Egypt down to the end of the Ptolemaic dynasty (31 B.C.) and after the land of Cleopatra was absorbed into the Roman Empire the glass-workers of Alexandria continued to ply their trade. Many of them emigrated to Rome where there was a ready market for their wares. To this period belong the beautiful glass bowls covered with millefiori decoration, which were fashionable with the Roman upper classes and which have been unearthed in many parts of the former Roman Empire. That the millefiori artists of the ancient world were held in high esteem is demonstrated by the fact that the businessmen of Alexandria erected a statue to Proculus of Perinthus who is said to have invented the multicoloured glass cane as we know it today, with a continuous pattern running throughout its entire length.

VENETIAN GLASS

Glass was manufactured all over the Roman Empire in the first centuries of the Christian era. In the Dark Ages which followed the 7

A small wheatflower
weight with a star-cut
base. 2 in.

disintegration of the empire in the fifth century glass-making virtually died out in Western Europe, but continued to flourish in the Eastern Empire, with its capital at Byzantium (Constantinople) and in Egypt, Anatolia and Syria under Arab domination. In 1204 Enrico Dandolo and a Venetian army captured Constantinople and occupied it till 1261. During that period many of the arts and crafts preserved by the Byzantines were imported into Venice and these included glass-making which rapidly developed as a Venetian industry in the thirteenth century. For five hundred years the glasshouses of the island of Murano exported fine crystal glass to all parts of Europe and Western Asia. Inevitably there was a revival of glass-making in Germany, France and other countries in the latter half of this period. As early as 1275 the Venetian authorities were passing regulations to forbid the export of glassmaking equipment and the emigration of glassworkers to other parts of Europe. The techniques of glass manufacture and the ingredients were kept closely guarded secrets in a vain attempt to preserve for Venice the monopoly of fine glass. The artistry and ingenuity of the Venetians was not sufficient to counter the competition. As the Venetian glass industry began to decline in the seventeenth century it was overtaken by the superior products of Bohemia, France and even England.

Nevertheless the importance of Venice in the history and development of glass in general and the paperweight in particular cannot be overlooked. To the Venetians is given the credit for reviving the Egyptian-Roman art of millefiori decoration, though the assertion that Venetian millefiori was being produced in the fourteenth century is now open to doubt. Several examples of Venetian millefiori glassware preserved in the Victoria and Albert Museum in London were once thought to date from the Renaissance, but recent research points to the likelihood of their manufacture in the seventeenth or eighteenth centuries. A few examples are recorded which may be Renaissance pieces but they are too few in number for any attempt at dating to be conclusive.

One cannot ignore, however, the statement of Marc Antonio Sabellico in his *De Situ Urbis Venetae* (c. 1495), relating to the manufacture of glass in his native Venice: "A famous invention first proved that glass might feign the whiteness of crystal, soon as the wits of men are active and not slothful in adding something to inventions, they began to turn the material into various colours and numberless forms . . . There is no kind of precious stone which cannot be imitated by the industry of the glassworkers, a sweet contest of nature and of man . . . But, consider to whom did it first occur to include in a little ball all the sorts of flowers which clothe the meadows in spring. Yet these things have been under the eyes of all nations as articles of export." This statement contains a number of tantalising features, not the least being the reference to a ball containing flowers. This has been taken to mean something approximating to the millefiori paperweights which became so popular in the mid-nineteenth century, but in the absence of Venetian paperweights of such an early date we must consider the alternatives. Glass balls, intended as hand-coolers, were being produced in the fifteenth century and it is possible that some of these incorporated millefiori ornament. Other experts, however, now consider that Sabellico was merely referring to the millefiori canes themselves and discount the possibility of glass balls being manufactured on a commercial scale, and certainly not for export as Sabellico implies. This passage from *De Situ Urbis Venetae* has been responsible for much of the inaccuracy and the misleading statements to be found in books dealing with Venetian glass, published in the eighteenth and nineteenth centuries. It must be remembered that, until George Ravenscroft perfected his lead glass in 1676, it would have been impossible to produce globes of glass of the flawless clarity required for paperweights. Moreover paper itself did not become a popular commodity until the eighteenth century and the need for weights to hold it down could not materialise until a later date. Thus we can firmly discount the possibility of glass paperweights dating from the Venetian Renaissance eventually turning up.

The Venetians also developed the style of decoration known as *latticinio*, in which threads of opaque (usually milk-white) glass were woven in a trellis pattern and embedded in a clear glass surround. This form of decoration was popular in the stems of wine-glasses and the handles of glass vessels manufactured in Venice from the sixteenth century onwards. Latticinio spread to other parts of Europe and was well-nigh universal in the seventeenth century. In paperweights it is used effectively for the grounds of individual flower weights, or to divide segments of millefiori.

Flowers and fruits made of glass were another Venetian speciality in the seventeenth and early eighteenth centuries, and these were to become a feature of the rarer paperweights of the nineteenth century, though there is no evidence to suggest that the Venetians ever enclosed these objects in glass globes.

In 1798 Napoleon Bonaparte suppressed the Most Serene Republic of Saint Mark and subsequently incorporated the Venetian territories into the Hapsburg empire. At the nadir of its political fortunes Venice suffered a recession of its trade and industry and at the beginning of the nineteenth century glassmaking

BELOW Pink clematis on a spiral latticinio ground. 3¼ in.

BOTTOM An upright bouquet weight by St Louis, surrounded by a white corkscrew and pink spirals on a star-cut base. 3¼ in.

9

A turquoise double-
overlay weight by
Baccarat with two
interlacing garlands
and animal canes.
3¼ in.

Patterned millefiori
weight. 3 in.

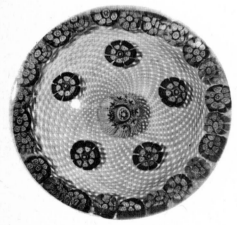

had almost died out. Its revival owed much to Pietro Bigaglia whose family had operated glasshouses on Murano since the late seventeenth century. Bigaglia diversified his activities from plate and mirror glass to include coloured glass lamps, decorative glassware and glass novelties which included paperweights.

In *Curiosities of Glass-Making* (1849) by Apsley Pellatt, whose own contribution to the art of the paperweight is noted later, Venetian balls produced in that decade are described as "a collection of waste pieces of filigree glass conglomerated together, without regular design: this is packed into a pocket of transparent glass, which is adhesively collapsed upon the interior mass by sucking up, producing outward pressure of the atmosphere." The earliest examples were cuboid or cylindrical and the characteristic rounded dome and flattened base did not materialise till later. Little attempt was made at a deliberate pattern of millefiori canes; they were all jumbled up together and tightly packed with little regard to aesthetic sensibility. Weights incorporating a dated cane have been recorded from 1845 onwards and it seems reasonable to suppose that such paperweights were being manufactured by Bigaglia, Franchini and their competitors from 1842 or 1843, since the dated weights are superior in technique and finish to some of the undated weights extant from this period. The Venetian weights were not as deep as those later perfected in France and elsewhere and little or no attempt was made to exploit the magnifying properties of the enclosing glass dome. The glass in Venetian weights tended to be opaque and lacked the high finish of the French weights. It never seems to have occurred to the Venetian manufacturers that the effect of the millefiori could be enhanced by magnification through the glass dome. This is true also of other Venetian novelties, such as vases, bowls and knobs, in which millefiori decoration was only lightly covered by clear glass.

In May 1845 an Exhibition of Austrian Industry was staged in Vienna. Venice, a part of the Austrian province of Lombardo-Venezia until its liberation in 1866, was represented at the exhibition and Bigaglia displayed examples of his millefiori paperweights. These attracted the attention of Eugéne Pèligot, of the *Conservatoire des Arts et Metiers* in Paris, who was present as an observer on behalf of the Paris Chamber of Commerce. Pèligot subsequently reported on the Venetian paperweights and it is generally accepted that he was responsible for their introduction to France. This now seems unlikely since the earliest dated weights of St Louis, for example, bear the year 1845 and by that time had far surpassed their Venetian counterparts. Weights, attributed to St Louis, are known in which the canes almost completely fill the dome in the

Venetian style and do not have the magnified characteristic of the later weights. From this it must be deduced that French weights were being produced before 1845.

BOHEMIAN GLASS

Glass was being manufactured in Bohemia and Silesia from the fourteenth century, if not earlier, and gradually ousted Venetian glass from the markets of Germany and northern Europe in the seventeenth century. Various suggestions for emulating Venetian millefiori decoration had been made in Germany in the late eighteenth century but it was not until 1833 that the Prussian authorities gave financial support to a project by Dr W. E. Fuss for the manufacture of millefiori glass at Hoffnungstal in Silesia. The venture was a commercial success and soon millefiori-decorated articles were being produced in other glasshouses of Silesia and Bohemia. Among the outstanding manufacturers in this field were F. Egermann at Antoniwald and Franz Pohl of the Josephine works. They produced all manner of glass objects covered with millefiori decoration in the Venetian style, but paperweights as such did not appear until the middle of the 1840s. The earliest dated weight is of 1848, but five years earlier the Bohemians were producing incrustations (discussed in the next chapter) and since the same technique of enfolding the decoration in clear glass was employed it is assumed that millefiori paperweights were made in Bohemia and Silesia by 1845 or 1846. The exact date has puzzled historians for some time and until more substantial evidence is produced it cannot be ascertained whether the Bohemians imitated the Venetians and the French or the other way round. It is surely significant that no mention of Bohemian paperweights is made in the reports of the Vienna exhibition of May 1845, though Bohemia (modern Czechoslovakia) formed part of the Habsburg dominions at that time.

A turquoise colour-ground weight by Clichy with a trefoil garland. 3¼ in.

The Bohemian paperweights of 1848 were technically the equal of those produced in France and point either to several years of gradual development, or the overnight emergence of a highly accomplished art form. Since millefiori decoration was used in bottle stoppers and other glass novelties from the mid-1830s it seems that the former conjecture is the more probable. Continuing research into the antecedents of paperweights indicates that these attractive baubles were being devised and developed in Italy, Bohemia and France more or less simultaneously and independently. The history of paperweights in these three countries, their characteristics, profiles and idiosyncrasies, are discussed at greater length in subsequent chapters.

11

Two
Sulphides and Incrustations

Although millefiori and latticinio decoration contribute the bulk of decorative motifs found in glass paperweights a large minority of weights form the important group known as sulphides or incrustations. Because their appearance and technique of production differs radically from that of most other paperweights it is more convenient to deal with them separately, and since they appeared before millefiori paperweights it is logical to discuss them first.

Sulphides are small medallions made of china clay, glass paste or some other opaque substance and though their use in paperweights dates only from about 1816 they were in existence long before that, either as objects in their own right, or embedded in glassware such as decanters and door-knobs. These charming little objects had their origins in the mid-eighteenth century and arose from a desire to imitate the cameos and intaglio gems of classical times.

Credit for inventing the glass-paste cameo is given to James Tassie (1735–99), a Glasgow stonemason who studied sculpture at the Glasgow Academy of Fine Arts. In 1763 he moved to Dublin where he was employed by Dr Henry Quin, King's Professor of Physics, in research into vitreous substances. Quin and Tassie perfected the 'white enamel composition' which the latter afterwards used to cast wax portraits modelled from the life. The formula of this vitreous paste was carefully guarded by Tassie and his nephew William, who succeeded him in the business, and the secret seems to have vanished with the death of the younger Tassie since no other modeller appears to have used it in more recent years.

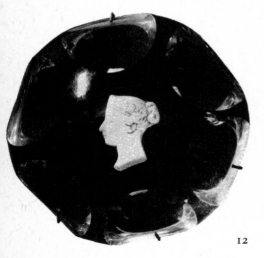

Large overlay weight (8¾ in. diameter) with 6 printies, portraying Queen Victoria.

James Tassie settled in London in 1766 and began his business of reproducing Greek and other antique engraved gems. He quickly established a reputation for the fine quality of his work and eventually he obtained ready access to the richest collections both in Britain and on the Continent. The London jewellers introduced the fashion of wearing Tassie gems set in rings, seals and other trinkets, and he found a ready sale for his reproductions. By 1769 he was also producing casts for Josiah Wedgwood; the majority of the cameos and intaglios in Wedgwood's first catalogue, published in 1773, were casts from moulds supplied by Tassie, though later Wedgwood was content to employ his own artists and something of the rivalry which developed between them can be gauged from Wedgwood's rather grudging reference to Tassie as "an admirable and an honourable man whom it is a credit to emulate, although his seals are not as good as mine". Tassie's own catalogue first appeared in 1775 and listed over 3,000 items. By 1783 his fame had spread as far as Russia, where the Empress Catherine commissioned a complete set of Tassie gems and cameos. This collection was catalogued by Rudolph Raspe, Keeper of the Museum of Antiquities at Cassel, and listed some 15,800 items, mainly reproductions of ancient gems.

But it is for his original medallion portraits that Tassie deserves to be remembered as a capable artist in his own right. Examples of these, which he modelled in wax, in most cases directly from life, and afterwards cast in his hard white enamel, were exhibited in the Royal Academy every year from 1769 to 1791 (except 1780). In the earliest examples only the heads and busts were executed in vitreous paste, being afterwards mounted on backgrounds of glass which was tinted by placing coloured papers beneath it. Subsequently, however, Tassie perfected the technique of casting portrait and background in one piece. As his biographer, John Gray, described the medallions, "There is a great variety of tone, texture and general effect. Sometimes he attains a porcelain-like colour and surface; at others, he imitates, with great beauty, the yellow tone and peculiar markings of time-mellowed ivory; or again he aims at the appearance of sculptor's marble, and reproduces its faint wandering lines of delicate blue." James and William Tassie produced upwards of 500 different contemporary portrait medallions. John Wilson also produced original portraits using a white vitreous paste from about 1765 onwards.

Small faceted weight portraying Benjamin Franklin on a turquoise ground.

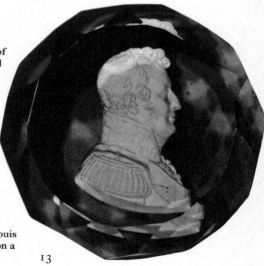

LEFT **Small Clichy sulphide with the conjoined profiles of Queen Victoria and Prince Albert on a clear ground. 2¾ in.**

RIGHT **Baccarat sulphide of King Louis Philippe (1830–48) on a blue ground. 3⅜ in.**

13

Large sulphide portrait
of King George III
(6 × 4½ in.), made
between 1825 and 1850.

Clichy blue-ground,
faceted weight
containing a sulphide
figure of Napoleon,
inside a garland of pink
and green roses with
circular 'windows'.
3½ in.

Tassie had a tremendous influence on the decorative glassware of Bohemia and his early experiments at embedding his cameos in glass were developed by the Bohemians towards the end of the eighteenth century. Glass objects in which were embedded clay or glass paste medallions began to appear in France in the 1790s, the Boileau factory at Gros-Caillou near Paris specialising in this form of decoration. Sulphides, as these glass-encrusted cameos became known, were very popular on the Continent from 1800 till about 1830 when they began to decline in fashion. Though primarily a European product they received their greatest impetus from the research of an English glass manufacturer, Apsley Pellatt, who patented his *crystallo-ceramie* process in 1819: "The figure intended for incrustation must be made of materials that will require a higher degree of heat for their fusion than the glass within which it is to be incrusted; these are china clay and super-silicate of potash, ground and mixed in such proportions as upon experiment harmonize with the density of the Glass."

Pellatt's contribution to the literature of glass-making was almost as prodigious as the techniques of glass production which he developed, describing the process by which he formed his sulphides in his book *Glass Manufactures*, published in 1821. "By the improved process", wrote Pellatt in another of his books, *Memoir on the Origins of Glassmaking*, "ornaments of any description, and landscapes of any variety of colour may be introduced into the glass. The substance of which they are composed is less fusible than glass and may previously be formed by either moulding or modelling, and it may be painted with enamel colours which are fixed by exposure to a melting heat. Specimens of these incrustations have been exhibited not only in decanters and wine-glasses, but in lamps, girandoles, chimney ornaments, plates and smelling bottles. Busts and statues on a small scale to support lamps and clocks and masks after the antique, have been introduced with admirable effect."

In 1831 Pellatt took out a patent on his mould for the manufacture of 'glazed pottery'. By using this mould he was able to cast cameos over which successive layers of molten glass could be poured to build up a paperweight. Sulphide paperweights by Apsley Pellatt were immensely popular in the nineteenth century. They may be found with intricate landscapes or portraying famous personalities. Queen Victoria and the Prince Consort were popular subjects for sulphide paperweights and, appropriately enough, the Crystal Palace, venue of the Great Exhibition of 1851, was another popular motif.

In France sulphides were produced by Saint-Amans and the

14

Parisian sculptor Desprez whose son began incrusting them in glass paperweights about 1819. The glasshouses of Mont-Cenis and Creusot manufactured sulphides in the early nineteenth century, long before Baccarat, Clichy and St Louis began making millefiori weights. The French artist Martoret produced a signed sulphide paperweight featuring the Great Exhibition of 1851, with the sky and lettering in pale blue. It is important to note, however, that such sulphide paperweights as were produced prior to the 1840s were of the flat rectangular type and bore little resemblance to the rounded globular weights of the 1840s and 1850s.

Baccarat sulphide of the Immaculate Conception on a ruby-red ground. 3¼ in.

Nevertheless, after the development of the glass paperweight in the 1840s it was inevitable that sulphides should be used as a decorative medium. Sulphide paperweights were produced by Baccarat and Clichy, but not St Louis, in the nineteenth century and these continued to be produced long after the millefiori weights went into decline. Nearly all of the Baccarat weights incrusted the sulphides on a plain background, whereas Clichy usually incorporated a border of millefiori canes. Baccarat produced sulphide portraits of all the popular heroes of the age – Napoleon Bonaparte, Napoleon III, the Duke of Orleans and King Louis Philippe with equal impartiality, Benjamin Franklin, George Washington, Czar Nicholas I, Pope Pius IX and Queen Victoria. Biblical subjects, the Virgin Mary and the saints were also popular subjects.

BELOW Sulphide weight portraying Robert Burns, Scotland's national poet, by John Ford of Edinburgh, mid 19th century. 3¼ in.

Almost as great was the range of sulphide weights which emanated from Clichy, but relatively few were produced by St Louis until recent times. From Clichy came sulphides portraying Chateaubriand, St Vincent de Paul, Alfred de Musset, Marie Antoinette, the Empress Eugenie and St Elizabeth, as well as some of the more popular figures which were also favoured by Baccarat. The Clichy sulphides were characterised by their coloured grounds, ranging from pale green to deep aquamarine and even black. The St Louis sulphides were set in clear glass and often had a laurel wreath round the profile. St Louis also favoured a carpet of tiny millefiori canes and made attractive use of overlays and facets. Unusual subjects for sulphides from this factory include bouquets of flowers and carp. St Louis produced a handsome sulphide weight in 1953 to celebrate the coronation of Queen Elizabeth, but this promising start was not followed up, and it was left to Baccarat to continue this tradition.

BELOW Mid 19th century English sulphide portraying William Shakespeare. 2¾ in.

Baccarat revived the art of sulphide paperweights in 1951, on the prompting of Paul Jokelson, the noted collector and author on paperweights. Mr Jokelson sent them a specimen of an Eisenhower presidential campaign medal and suggested that they use this as the basis of a sulphide weight. After many attempts Baccarat 15

Sulphide medallion of
an unknown French
officer, wearing the
Order of St. Esprit and
medals, with a green
glass background. 3½ in.

finally succeeded in making a sulphide which was artistically poor but which withstood the temperature of the molten glass and its cooling without cracking or yellowing. Only 153 Eisenhower weights were manufactured, unfacetted, on a bluish ground. They were so unattractive that they hardly sold. Now they are highly prized as the prototype of the present boom in sulphide weights. Jokelson urged Baccarat to make a paperweight in honour of the coronation of Queen Elizabeth in June 1953. Conjoined profiles of Queen Elizabeth and Prince Philip were sculpted by Gilbert Poillerat and cast as sulphides for a paperweight released in a limited edition of 1,492 regular and 195 overlay weights. The success of this weight was the turning point, and since that date Baccarat have produced an impressive range of portrait paperweights.

As the bulk of the Baccarat weights are now intended for the American market the majority of the subjects depicted have an American connection – Washington, Franklin, Lincoln, Jefferson, Robert E. Lee and more recent personalities such as John F. Kennedy and Sam Rayburn. A Franco-American note was struck by the issuance of a paperweight portraying the Marquis de Lafayette in 1959, to mark the bicentenary of his birth. Other weights have portrayed Popes Pius XII and John XXIII, though a religious balance was struck by producing a weight depicting Martin Luther. The most recent sulphides have all portrayed prominent Americans – Theodore Roosevelt, the humorist Will Rogers, Presidents James Monroe and Herbert Hoover, the statesman Adlai Stevenson and Eleanor Roosevelt, best remembered for her work in the field of International Human Rights. The size of the editions has risen slightly over the years and now stands at an average of 2,500 in the regular edition and 400 in the overlay edition. The same techniques have been applied to an unlimited edition of twelve sulphide weights featuring the signs of the zodiac. The motifs were sculpted by Poillerat based on drawings by Raphael and originally appeared in 1955 in a limited edition of 150 of each, on a pale blue ground. Subsequently they have been issued in unlimited quantities on a cobalt blue ground.

BRITISH SULPHIDES

Curiously enough the companies who made sulphide weights never produced millefiori weights, and the glasshouses who specialised in the latter never turned their attention to sulphide weights. Apart from Apsley Pellatt's Falcon glasshouse, which produced 'letter weights' from about 1821 to 1840, the best sulphide weights were made by Allen & Moore, William Kidd of London, Oslers of Birmingham, Lloyd & Summerfield of Birmingham and

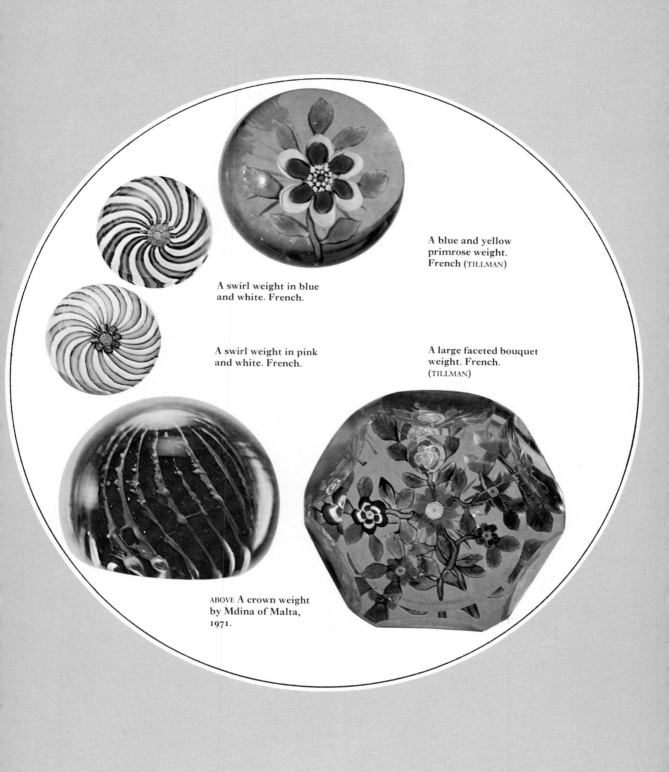

A swirl weight in blue
and white. French.

A blue and yellow
primrose weight.
French (TILLMAN)

A swirl weight in pink
and white. French.

A large faceted bouquet
weight. French.
(TILLMAN)

ABOVE A crown weight
by Mdina of Malta,
1971.

ST LOUIS

Carpet-ground weight with a sulphide portrait of Queen Victoria. (TILLMAN)

A moulded pink salamander. The only other recorded example of this weight is in the Bergstrom Museum. (TILLMAN)

ABOVE A strawberry weight with a single yellow-centred white flower, flanked by Alpine strawberries on a double spiral latticinio ground

A very rare pink camomile and pansy weight on a cushion of overlapping latticinio spirals.

John Ford of Edinburgh. The range of portraits was fairly limited, the manufacturers concentrating on members of the British royal family and prominent politicians of the mid-nineteenth century such as Robert Peel and the Duke of Wellington. There were many sulphides with neo-classical themes and several versions of the Crystal Palace of the 1851 Exhibition are recorded in British sulphide weights. Though not sulphide weights in the strict sense there were portrait medallions in glass paperweights, the profile appearing intaglio. This effect was created apparently by impressing a relief of a portrait in the still-molten glass which was then dipped in hydrofluoric acid. Oslers, among others, specialised in this unusual form of glass paperweight.

AMERICAN SULPHIDES

There are many examples of sulphide paperweights emanating from the United States in the second half of the nineteenth century but except in a small number of instances it is impossible to attribute these weights to particular factories with any certainty. The New England Glass Company is credited with the bulk of the production, though this has never been proved satisfactorily. Other firms which are known to have made sulphides include Bakewell of Pittsburgh who were producing them as early as 1839. In general American sulphides are relatively crude in appearance and the quality of the background and the surrounding glass is poor. Apart from the ubiquitous Queen Victoria the most popular subjects were American politicians and military heroes of the Indian wars and the Civil War. A few of them merely portrayed unidentified beauties and were the sort of tawdry and gimcrack novelties which would have been distributed as fairground prizes. Nevertheless they have a certain quaint, naive appeal and consequently are now eagerly snapped up by American collectors. Few of these weights ever found their way to Europe. In the modern paperweight revival sulphides seem to have been entirely neglected by the American manufacturers.

SULPHIDES OF OTHER COUNTRIES

Although the Bohemian glasshouses were in the forefront of paperweight production, and though sulphides were produced for incorporation in stoppers, wine goblets and door knobs, the Bohemians never seem to have produced sulphides as paperweights. After Bohemia became part of the independent republic of Czechoslovakia, however, there was a belated revival of interest in incrustations and some attractive sulphide paperweights appeared in the 1920s and 1930s. Czech sulphides are characterised by their high

Sulphide plaque by Apsley Pellatt, portraying an unidentified gentleman. 4⅛ in.

Baccarat *crystalloceramie* faceted weight showing a hunting scene. 3¼ in.

19

domes and the distinctive yellow-brown tinge of the glass which was a hallmark of classic Bohemian weights. The subjects were invariably animals and birds, in an upright, three-dimensional treatment. Like Czech paperweights in general, these sulphides had the overall pattern of facets which gives them an unusual appearance.

A few nineteenth century sulphide paperweights have been recorded with portraits of kings, queens and popular figures suggesting Belgian or Scandinavian manufacture. Virtually nothing is known about these weights and there is always the possibility that they were produced in France for export to these countries. Both Belgium and Sweden, however, have lengthy traditions of glass-making, so the possibility of native manufacture cannot be ruled out. Though the Kosta and Orrefors glasshouses of Sweden have been producing excellent and unusual paperweights in recent years neither of them has experimented with sulphides so far.

ABOVE A D'Albret overlay weight of Leonardo da Vinci. (TILLMAN)

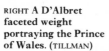

RIGHT A D'Albret faceted weight portraying the Prince of Wales. (TILLMAN)

BELOW A D'Albret overlay sulphide weight of Mark Twain. (TILLMAN)

ABOVE Baccarat overlay weight portraying Queen Elizabeth II and Prince Philip. (TILLMAN)

LEFT An overlay weight of Christopher Columbus by D'Albret. (TILLMAN)

20

Three

Venetian Paperweights

Glass paperweights were first produced in Venice about 1843 and had passed their peak within a decade, though they continued to be produced sporadically for many years and have been revived in recent years to serve the tourist market.

The classic Venetian weights came in a wide variety of shapes and did not always have the flattened base characteristic of other paperweights. Their main feature, however, was the relative shallowness of the dome, so that little use was made of the magnifying properties of the clear glass. The quality of the glass was not as high as that used in Bohemia or France. The glass was soda-lime in composition and often tinted or semi-opaque in appearance. The surface of the weight was often rough and speckled, and generally lacked the finish of the French weights. The millefiori canes were closely packed in a scrambled formation, and little attempt was made at deliberate patterns. Later weights had the canes more evenly spaced.

The canes in these early weights were limited in design and composition, based on plain or crimped tubes, stars and cogs. The canes were relatively simple, consisting of up to six narrow rods, though a notable exception was a cane composed of very thin rods arranged in a circle on the Roman millefiori pattern. The colours were, for the most part, rather garish and lifeless.

The venetian weights were noted for their silhouette canes, of which there was a wide variety. As these help to identify the weights they are worth mentioning in some detail. Human figures include a negro in striped trousers and a running figure who may have been intended to represent the devil. The animal silhouettes include a horse, a white goat, a crouching dog and a pelican. Other subjects are a gondola, a chessboard and the railway causeway whose construction to Venice was completed in 1846. There is a number of canes with the profiles of people, mainly ladies, though there was a brief resurgence of portrait canes for patriotic reasons in the late 1860s and weights incorporating tiny profiles of Garibaldi, Cavour and other popular heroes date from that period. Several weights are recorded with lettering on the canes. Those inscribed PB and GBF identify Bigaglia and Franchini who manufactured the weights, but others – FC, AC, B, R, MR and CW have not been positively identified. A weight of 1846 bears the initials FI (*Ferdinand Imperator*) and the Austrian imperial arms. Dated weights are comparatively rare, though canes bearing dates from 1845 to

Close-packed millefiori Venetian weight, dated 1846, with initial B cane.

1848 are known. An interesting and unusual weight even has a cane inscribed in full with the name of the ninth Congress of Scientists held in Venice in 1847.

Bigaglia exhibited at the Great Exhibition of 1851, but seems to have turned away from glass paperweights after that date. Though weights were no longer produced, the Venetians continued to make glass objects with millefiori decoration. Apart from Bigaglia and Franchini, other companies who specialised in this type of glassware included Salviati and the Venezia-Murano Company who also concentrated on bowls, vases and even knife-handles decorated with millefiori rather than making paperweights as such. Venetian millefiori continued in a desultory fashion, never attaining the brilliance of the French or the technical excellence of the Americans. There was a revival of interest in paperweights in the period between the two world wars and the Murano glasshouses obligingly turned out large quantities of poor quality weights distinguished by raw,

A group of mid 19th century objects with typical Venetian millefiori decoration of the period. Note the silhouette canes of gondolas on the lids of the 2 boxes.

garish colours in the small canes set in close concentric circles.

The output of paperweights was briefly suspended during the Second World War, but by 1950 vast quantities of cheap weights were being exported to America. These weights can usually be recognised by their large cogged canes in violent shades of red, blue, yellow, orange or green. By the early 1960s, however, the quality of Venetian paperweights had begun to improve; the colours were in muted and delicate shades, and the clarity of the glass was much better. They are now manufactured in a wide variety of shapes and sizes, ranging from miniatures to door-stop magnums, and depart from the conventional shape to include rectangles, cubes and even book-ends. As well as the millefiori weights (whose patterns are more imaginative now than their nineteenth century counterparts) Venice is producing attractive flower and fish weights and among the more recent products are weights incorporating the coats of arms of Italian cities. The leading manufacturers of paperweights on Murano today are

Venetian millefiori decoration on seals, scent bottles, mirrors, brooches and paperweights, 1846–7.

Venetian glass bowl
of the 16th century
($3\frac{1}{2}$ in. diameter)
incorporating
millefiori canes.

Pauly, Venini and Gilliano Ferro. The better quality weights are exported to the United States and other countries,and it is unfortunate that the actual visitor to Murano is likely to be fobbed off with second-rate material.

Murano has recently departed from traditional forms and begun experimenting with new shapes. Among those noted are a melon-rib moulded glass weight enclosing a concentric millefiori cushion. Another type, known in the trade as a 'dimplex' may be described as a tall rounded rectangle with concavities in the four sides and the top. These weights enclose flower or millefiori patterns. From *SVCC Vetri d'Arte* of Murano come large egg-shaped weights with an opaque overlay and two circular printies through which a single blue cane can be viewed in solitary splendour.

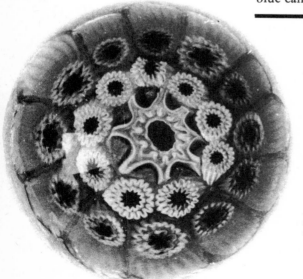

Modern Muranese
concentric millefiori
weight.

Four

Bohemian Paperweights

Relatively little attention has been paid to the paperweights of Bohemia and it is only within the past decade that they have received the recognition they deserve. Millefiori decoration was incorporated in glassware of all kinds from the middle 1830s, largely as a result of Venetian influence and a desire to emulate and compete with Murano. In addition credit must be given to General Heinrich von Minutoli, an amateur archaeologist and collector of glass, who unearthed examples of Roman millefiori in Bohemia and urged the glasshouses of Bohemia and Silesia to produce similar work.

The Bohemian glasshouses differed from the Venetian in at least one notable respect; they had a penchant for enamel painting and sulphide incrustation (see Chapter 2). Millefiori paperweights were in production by 1846 if not earlier and more closely resemble the French weights than the Venetian. It is likely that Bohemia influenced France, and vice versa, and there was a considerable two-way traffic in ideas and techniques in paperweight production in the 1840s.

The glasshouses of Bohemia favoured a lime-potash glass which was harder and lighter than lead glass and usually had a faint yellowish tinge. The Bohemian weights had a conventional profile, with a flat base with a slight concavity, the sides bulging over the base and a relatively low dome. Overlay weights, with a flat top and windows ground into the sides, had a higher dome and a plain flat base. The overlays provided a number of facets through which the interior of the weight could be viewed from different angles.

The millefiori canes used by the Bohemian and Silesian manufacturers were, like the Venetians of the same period, relatively simple in design and composition. Plain or crimped tubes, bundles of thin rods of contrasting colours, stars and florets made up the repertoire of Bohemian cane shapes. The range of colours and shades was far greater than the Venetian and the colours were generally softer and lighter. As with the Venetian weights the silhouette canes are a useful means of identification. They include the German eagle or the Austrian double-headed eagle, white rabbit, red rabbit, bee, dog, horse and white monkey. The only human figure is a dancing devil. A characteristic device is the cabbage rose which figures prominently and frequently in Bohemian weights. Only one date has so far been recorded in Bohemian paperweights – 1848, the year of revolutions. These dated weights are sometimes found with the letter 'j' above the date, though the significance of this letter has never been deduced. It may be a reference to the Josephine works, or merely be the abbreviated form for *Jahr* (year).

The majority of the Bohemian paperweights are of the millefiori type, with the canes scattered haphazardly on a white filigree ground which has the appearance of muslin. This scattered millefiori technique was also applied to other decorative articles such as vases and bottles in which the base resembled a paperweight. Bohemia also produced a few weights in which the decoration consisted of concentric circles of millefiori canes arranged inside a basket effect. Canes arranged in the centre of a swirling pattern are very rare in Bohemian weights; they have a rose or silhouette cane in the centre, with a circle of millefiori canes on a ground composed of white and pink swirling stripes. A few of these swirl weights have the very high-domed appearance of crown paperweights.

Bohemia also produced a number of overlay weights and these were generally smaller and higher-crowned than their French contemporaries. 'Printies', as the little windows ground in the sides and top of the weight are called, were often numerous, and arranged in double rows, creating an overall effect. The interior of overlay weights was similar to that of the regular weights, a scattered or concentric millefiori pattern on a muslin ground. These weights have often been confused with the overlay weights of Baccarat, but their relative smallness and the lightness of the glass, together with the distinctive yellowish tinge of Bohemian glass, should aid identification.

At least one high-domed basket weight has been attributed to Bohemia on the grounds of the type of glass and the style of millefiori canes. This rare item passed through Sotheby's saleroom some

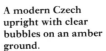

A modern Czech upright with clear bubbles on an amber ground.

years ago and no other basket weight of this type from Bohemia has so far come to light.

The manufacture of glass paperweights in Bohemia seems to have come to an end in 1849. The turbulent political events of that year may have been a contributing factor. Paperweight manufacture was not, in fact, resumed until the early 1920s when the republic of Czechoslovakia revived many of the traditional arts and crafts of Bohemia. The sulphide weights of this period have already been mentioned in Chapter 2, but the Czech glasshouses also produced millefiori weights consciously imitating the classic weights of the 1840s, without much success. They had more success with the tall, multi-facetted weights incorporating flowers and also dabbled with a series of tall portrait weights incorporating transfer-printed photographs of Masaryk and other patriots of the struggle for independence. These pictures were mounted on a two-dimensional ceramic base and appear upright within the weights. These weights were designed to meet popular patriotic demand in the 1920s and had little aesthetic appeal. Since the Second World War however, the glasshouses of Bohemia have returned once more to the subject of paperweights and are now concentrating on high-domed, multifacetted flower weights in the style of the late 1920s. The execution of the flowers is competent and the colours are usually quite attractive, but the glass itself leaves room for improvement.

The most recent development has been the production of fruit weights, redolent of the blown fruit weights of the New England Glass Company in the nineteenth century. Unlike their American predecessors the modern Czech versions are free standing, their bottoms being suitably flattened, whereas the American fruit weights were mounted on a 'cookie' base. The Czech fruit weights are to be found in translucent glass of various colours, with blue, green and ruby-red predominating. Many of them are of clear glass throughout but others have an attractive aerated effect in the lower half which often has the appearance of a cushion ground. The Czech glasshouses have also produced a number of moulded glass weights in the shape of animals and birds. This idiom had no counterpart in the classic period, though it may derive inspiration from the moulded glass figures popularised by the Heisey Glass Company of Newark, Ohio, in the nineteenth century. Heisey's moulds and equipment were acquired by the Imperial Glass Corporation of Bellaire, Ohio, which recommenced their production in 1958. The Heisey figures are not paperweights but free standing objects, whereas the animals and birds manufactured in Czechoslovakia and other European countries today have the characteristic heavy base indicating their purpose.   27

Five

French Paperweights

To most people, whether they are collectors or not, paperweights mean French paperweights, and French paperweights mean the products of Baccarat, Clichy and St Louis. The great bulk of literature on the subject of glass paperweights is devoted to the work of these three factories, and rightly so, for their output was spectacular in quantity and quality and has never been surpassed anywhere else in the world. Each of the three major factories produced paperweights of outstanding beauty and distinction and, because they have highly individual characteristics, they are the subject of separate chapters which analyse their work in greater detail. At this point, however, some general remarks on the history and development of glass manufacture in France are appropriate, with particular reference to paperweights, and the claims put forward for other factories are examined.

Compared with Bohemia-Silesia and Venice, eighteenth century France did not figure among the leading producers of glass. A certain amount of plate glass was manufactured in the country, but much of the decorative wares had to be imported from Venice or Bohemia. At the end of the eighteenth century there were barely fifty glasshouses in operation in the whole of France, but in thirty years this number had almost quadrupled and glass-manufacturing had risen to become one of the country's most important industries, a position which it holds to this day.

Not only did glass production in the first half of the nineteenth century rise astronomically but the range and quality of products increased enormously. There was an aggressive, zestful atmosphere in the French glass industry in the 1830s and 1840s and an intense eagerness to try anything new. Millefiori, sulphides and glass paperweights might have originated elsewhere but these techniques and art forms were readily seized by the French and developed with a thoroughness and intensity which is nothing short of dramatic. Almost overnight the French glasshouses took hold of an insignificant bauble of mixed Venetian and Bohemian parentage, improved on it beyond all recognition and produced objects of great beauty at a time when the applied and decorative arts in general were approaching their nadir of tastelessness. Largely as a result of the activities of Baccarat, Clichy and St Louis, the glass paperweight stands out in the Victorian wilderness as a redeeming feature of that philistine age.

Why the paperweights of France should suddenly have appeared

A very rare, but
unidentified faceted
weight containing a
swan on a pond with a
star-cut base. 3¼ in.

An extremely rare
yellow-ground
magnum weight
depicting a blue
butterfly of unusual
form. Tentatively
attributed to Baccarat.
3¾ in.

An unidentified black
salamander weight.
3⅞ in.

ABOVE A fine garland
weight on a rose-
coloured ground. 3¼ in.

29

to the world in their highly developed and exquisite form is a mystery which can never be satisfactorily explained, nor why, having attained such perfection, they should have vanished from the scene so rapidly. Moreover, the French factories were not content to produce standard millefiori or sulphide weights, but experimented with different sizes, from miniatures to magnums, mushrooms and overlays, flower and fruit weights and such *recherché* types as *marbrie* and salamander weights.

The three following chapters deal with the main French factories and their products, but the question of other factories has never been satisfactorily resolved. On the one hand there are many French weights whose origins are not known for certain, and on the other hand, there are references to the manufacture of paper-weights at various glasshouses, other than the big three. The identity of these weights, tying them in with factories reputed to have produced weights, has not so far been ascertained, but the references are given here for what they are worth.

In 1849 the Paris Exposition, forerunner of London's Great Exhibition of 1851, coincided with the heyday of the paperweight and it is not surprising that the *Journal of Design and Manufactures* published that year should have made copious reference to these articles, with somewhat confusing and misleading results. One of these concerns the glasshouse of St Maude: "The works at St Maude rather confine themselves to the speciality of Venetian glass, more particularly as applied to those fanciful objects which swarm in the windows of the shops of the Palais Royal and on the dressing tables of the upper classes. To descend from gay to grave, from lively to serene, from elegance to comfort, from paperweights to wine bottles . . ." From this tantalising snippet we might infer that the factory of St Maude produced paperweights, but all attempts to substantiate this statement have had negative results.

A rare cherry weight on a clear ground, possibly Pantin. 3 in.

The brilliance of Baccarat, Clichy and St Louis has blinded students to the possibilities of other factories and it is only within recent years that attention is being given to this possibility. Perhaps some documentary evidence will turn up which will confirm or deny the St Maude theory.

The same Journal contains the more positive reference to "The establishment of M. Bontemps at Choisy-le-Roi. It is a great centre of activity, and to him the Parisians are indebted for their supply of all the thousand and one imitations and originalities which decorate their chimney pieces and sideboards." And in the *Art Journal* of the same year there is the following statement, "In France at the manufactory of Choisy-le-Roi under the able super-intendence of M. Bontemps, have been produced some clever imitations of millefiori fused in crystal glass; in one article alone, *viz.* paperweights, they have distributed over Europe hundreds of thousands of these elegant table ornaments." These irresponsible remarks were anonymous and students of French paperweight production have never been able to trace this *canard* back to its original source. 'Hundreds of thousands' would have been an exaggeration in describing the total French output, let alone that of a relatively obscure factory. Besides, by 1849 the Choisy-le-Roi glasshouse was very much in decline and Bontemps himself had left France, to work in England on the problems of developing glass lenses. All of his subsequent work was in the field of optics, so it is highly unlikely that Bontemps, who is sometimes associated with the introduction or revival of millefiori decoration in France, had much to do with the manufacture of paperweights.

An unusual portrait weight with a red velvet base.

The third of the problematical French factories was Pantin, known by various names between its foundation in 1850 and the adoption of its present name in 1900. In 1878, at the time of the *Exposition Universelle* in Paris, the company was known as Monot, Pere et Fils et Stumpf and as such exhibited glass and paperweights at the exposition. Evidence for the Pantin claim rests largely on the report prepared by Charles Colné, assistant secretary to the United States Commissioners for the Exposition: "Paperweights of solid glass, containing glass snakes, lizards, squirrels and flowers; air bubbles are distributed in the mass, looking like pearl drops . . . A coiled snake, with head erect, of two coloured glasses, cut in spots to show both colours, mounted on a piece of mirror; an interesting piece of workmanship, showing great dexterity in coiling the snake . . . Paperweights in millefiori of roses, leaves and fruit, embedded in lumps of clear glass . . . a paperweight containing a lizard of coloured glass, which had been cut in several parts before being inclosed in the glass."

This fairly detailed description has tempted many collectors and dealers into ascribing to Pantin a number of unidentified French weights which, on account of their three-dimensional motifs, seem to be of late nineteenth century manufacture. It is now generally realised, however, that the *Exposition Universelle* of 1878 stimulated something of a revival of interest in glass paperweights and it is likely that several glasshouses, including the Pantin establishment, dabbled in this field, perhaps as late as the outbreak of the First World War, though these weights may have been in the category of 'end of day' work, executed by craftsmen in their spare time.

Six
Baccarat Paperweights

A glasshouse known as the *Verrerie de St Anne* was established on the bank of the River Meurthe at Baccarat in the Vosges region of Alsace in 1764. The prime mover in this enterprise was a local clergyman, the Monseigneur de Montmorency-Laval, and the company was concerned primarily with the manufacture of plate glass, mirrors, bottles and utilitarian glassware. In 1816 the glasshouse amalgamated with the company run by D'Artigues, formerly director of the St Louis factory, and three years later began to produce fine lead glass. In 1822 D'Artigues sold his interest in the firm to a consortium of businessmen who renamed it the *Compagnie des Cristalleries de Baccarat*. Ten years later Baccarat conspired with its rival, St Louis, to buy up the Creusot glassworks. From then onwards Baccarat and St Louis were recognised as the two leading glasshouses in France, a position which they occupy to this day.

Baccarat displayed its wares at the Parisian expositions of 1844 and 1849, but no mention is made in the catalogue and reports of paperweights in connection with this company, although by the time of the latter exhibition Baccarat was pre-eminent in this field. Baccarat also exhibited in 1855, but again there is no mention of paperweight production and it is thought that this phase of the company's activities was drawing to a close by that date. At the *Exposition Universelle* of 1878 Baccarat received one of the Grand Medals for its glass products generally and Colné's report makes no mention of paperweights in connection with this firm. On the eve of the First World War the company claimed to have no craftsmen in its employment who could produce millefiori canes, yet twenty years later they were employing an old man named Dupont who made some excellent millefiori paperweights which were subsequently retailed at a little shop in Paris. After Dupont's death in 1934 the sale of these weights ceased. The motive in producing these weights is a little suspect, since many of them contain dated canes with ridiculous dates well before the 1840s. Though typically Baccarat in appearance these Dupont weights generally have smaller canes than the classic originals.

In 1951, while repairs were being carried out on the parish church of Baccarat, severely damaged by bombing in the Second World War, a Baccarat paperweight dated 1853 was discovered under the cornerstone. This triggered off a revival of millefiori paperweight production and since then, as noted at the end of this chapter,

A rare patterned millefiori weight on an upset muslin ground. 3¼ in.

A characteristic Baccarat primrose, a red and white striped flower in clear glass. 3⅛ in.

Baccarat has been in the forefront of the European paperweight revival.

The classic Baccarat weights do not have such deeply bulging sides as those of the other French factories, notably Clichy. The flat or slightly concave base of Baccarat weights is often decorated with a star motif which was distinctive to this factory. A relatively high proportion of Baccarat weights bear an initial B and a date. Dates found in Baccarat weights are 1846, 1847, 1848, 1849, 1853 and 1858, the last being regarded as an exceptional instance. The figures and letters appear in red, green or blue on white canes and there is an enormous variety of styles and combinations in which these dates appear. Though no weights of earlier dates have been found it is certain that Baccarat was manufacturing weights in 1845, if not earlier, since even the earliest dated examples are far superior to the Venetian and Bohemian weights of the same period.

Regular production of paperweights may have ceased in 1849, since the isolated cases of dates after that are all found on weights produced as mementoes of historic events – the cornerstone weight of 1853 and the close millefiori weights of 1858 celebrating the visit of Marshal Canrobert to Baccarat in April 1858.

Baccarat produced a wide variety of types of millefiori canes, of

ABOVE A mauve clematis with a garland border on a star-cut base. 3⅛ in.

BELOW A rare garland weight with a wall-flower and clematis centre-piece. 3¼ in.

BOTTOM A pansy and garland weight on a star-cut base. 3¼ in.

LEFT An unusual millefiori wafer stand with the Baccarat initial B and date 1848. 4 in.

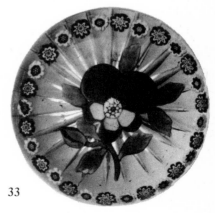

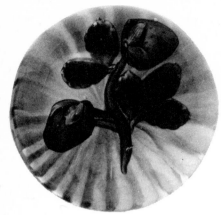

which a few were distinctive to that glasshouse. These were a curious star with six large and six small points and a large circle of colour in the centre, an open spiral whorl, double trefoil and quatrefoil, a three-pronged arrowhead and the so-called fortress or castle cane composed of four circular rods joined with a rectangular device in the centre. There was a good range of silhouette canes and these are most helpful in identifying Baccarat weights. The animals include dog, horse, goat, deer, monkey, elephant and squirrel; birds include stork, cockerel, swan, pheasant, pelican, pigeon and love-birds; other silhouettes include a huntsman, dancing devil and a moth, as well as several floral canes which are masterpieces of minute perfection.

Relatively few scattered millefiori weights were produced at Baccarat and seem to belong to the earlier phase in the production of paperweights. Close millefiori weights were a Baccarat speciality and are recorded with every date and in every size. These weights are absolutely crammed with millefiori and silhouette canes. Spaced millefiori weights have the canes widely separated and mounted on a ground of white filigree creating the impression of muslin. These weights show the Baccarat millefiori to best advantage and rank among the most attractive items from this factory. The majority of them belong to the middle period of production, from 1847 to 1849. Concentric weights contain two, three or four concentric circles of millefiori canes on a translucent ground or, occasionally a muslin ground which is sometimes mistaken for Clichy. In the Baccarat weights, however the muslin strands run counter clockwise, whereas the Clichy weights show the twists in a clockwise direction. Baccarat produced a number of weights in which the millefiori canes were arranged in two intertwining trefoils to form a garland. Most of them are found with clear grounds, but a few are on coloured or muslin grounds. There was also a single garland type with the canes forming a six-petalled pattern with a single cane placed near the point of each petal. A few unusual patterns are associated with this factory, including large composite patterns of concentric circles, interspersed with latticinio decoration and repeated silhouette motifs. These unusual patterns are so rare that definite conclusions cannot be formed about them.

Apart from the standard shapes Baccarat specialised in mushroom weights, aptly named on account of their high crown surrounded by a broader base. Millefiori canes were crowded into the upper tuft and pleasing patterns of latticinio spirals arranged round the lower part of the weight. The various patterns may also be found with overlays. Some of the concentric weights have a printy

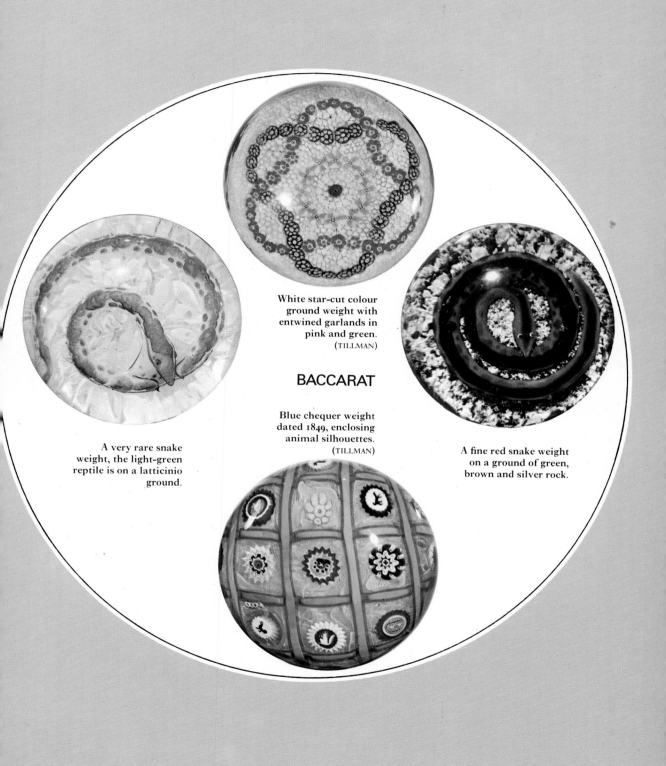

White star-cut colour ground weight with entwined garlands in pink and green.
(TILLMAN)

BACCARAT

Blue chequer weight dated 1849, enclosing animal silhouettes.
(TILLMAN)

A very rare snake weight, the light-green reptile is on a latticinio ground.

A fine red snake weight on a ground of green, brown and silver rock.

BACCARAT

Magnum patterned millefiori weight with entwined trefoil garland enclosing animals on a white latticinio ground.
(TILLMAN)

A rare magnum weight with a cruciform sunray base.

A superb magnum bouquet with a star-cut base.

ABOVE A very rare flat tricolour bouquet with 3 periwinkles on a star-cut base.

36

RIGHT A rare butterfly and wheatflower weight, the insect hovering over a yellow double clematis.

BELOW An intricate garland of millefiori on a pink ground. (SPINK & SON)

ABOVE An extremely rare yellow and blue clematis weight on a star-cut base.

ABOVE A most unusual crown imperial weight with 3 pendant orange bell-shaped flowers. Only 2 or 3 examples of this type of weight are known to exist.

RIGHT A flat bouquet weight with a pink thousand-petalled rose and a yellow wheat-flower. (TILLMAN)

BACCARAT

BACCARAT

TOP LEFT A fine rose weight, the pink cabbage rose formed of tightly packed, concentric petals.

CENTRE A yellow double clematis flanked by 2 buds. (TILLMAN)

ABOVE A fine mushroom weight of close-packed millefiori surrounded by blue and white latticinio. (SPINK & SON)

TOP RIGHT Scattered canes, including animal silhouettes, on a muslin ground. (SPINK & SON)

ABOVE An apple weight on a clear glass ground. (SPINK & SON)

LEFT A large faceted bouquet weight. (TILLMAN)

38

ground into the top to reduce the size of the pattern inside rather than magnify it. Facetting of this sort was often used in conjunction with mushroom weights. Attractive combinations of tiny millefiori canes produced the carpet grounds for which Baccarat was renowned. Conversely there was a limited variety of coloured grounds, other than those used for sulphide weights, the predominant colours being red, blue or green. Baccarat produced very few bouquet weights compared with St Louis. Those attributed to this glasshouse had deep facetting in the lower part to emphasise the bouquet effect.

Like the other French factories Baccarat produced a fine range of flower weights. Baccarat flowers were always stylised and seldom made concessions to naturalism. The same leaf pattern was used for all flowers, regardless of species, and a small millefiori cane usually served as the centre of the flower. Pansies were by far the most popular flower chosen by Baccarat and experts recognised three different types of pansy from this factory, all more or less contemporaneous. In descending order of popularity Baccarat favoured primroses, clematis, wheatflower, bellflowers, gentian and, rarest of all, a lavender-coloured dahlia. These flowers were rendered in a flat, two-dimensional manner, but in addition Baccarat produced some large weights in which the flowers were depicted in an upright, three-dimensional format. Different flowers were selected for this purpose – buttercup, camomile and rose – all of which are among the rarest of Baccarat weights. A few large weights also incorporated flat posies of flowers.

Baccarat manufactured a few fruit weights, of which their strawberry is the most distinctive. These weights contain three berries as a rule, one of which is unripe, and this effect was created by coating the berry with a light wash of green glass. The berries themselves were cunningly devised from a bundle of opaque white rods with red centres, rolled in such a way that the red points show up like the pores of the fruit. Other fruits which are rarely encountered are pears and apricots. Snakes and butterflies accounted for a minute portion of the Baccarat output. The butterflies may be found on a muslin ground, with a millefiori border or on a clear ground and incorporated with a flower motif.

Imbert and Amic, in *Les Presse-Papiers Français de Cristal*, assert that Baccarat was making large paperweights towards the end of the nineteenth century, with a lizard motif. As has already been noted in the previous chapter Charles Colné mentioned lizard weights by Pantin in 1878, though he does not mention paperweights by Baccarat at the same time. Consequently collectors are divided as to the identity of these lizard weights. Imbert and Amic

ABOVE A buttercup and garland weight on a turquoise ground. 2½ in.

BELOW A pompom miniature weight. 2¾ in.

CENTRE A rare pear weight on a clear glass ground. 2⅝ in.

BOTTOM A very fine butterfly and primrose weight. 3 in.

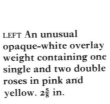

LEFT A fine *bouquet d' marriage* weight on a white spiral gauze with blue spirals at the base 2¾ in.

LEFT An unusual opaque-white overlay weight containing one single and two double roses in pink and yellow. 2⅝ in.

ABOVE The *Legion d'Honneur* surrounded by a garland in a weight with star-cut base and geometric sides. 3 in.

LEFT Faceted periwinkle with 6 printies and a star-cut base. 2½ in.

BELOW A dark-blue overlay weight with 7 windows in blue and white overlay with traces of gilding. 3 in.

LEFT A very rare star motif, the clear glass set with a disc of blue over a white field of stars, a window on top and two bands of printies. 2⅞ in.

40

even refer to a Baccarat price-list of 1907 in which lizard paperweights are catalogued. To add further to the confusion collectors have erroneously dubbed these reptiles salamanders, though the paperweight versions have the scales and skin markings usually associated with lizards. Hollister adds an American touch and refers to those with short bodies and fat tails as gila monsters. Whatever their correct zoological definition these Baccarat/Pantin reptiles are among the rarest and most highly regarded of all paperweights. The great Maba salamander weight, attributed to St Louis but just as likely to have been made at Baccarat or Pantin, was sold at Sotheby's in 1963 for £3,900 ($9,360) and fetched £6,000 ($14,400) in the same salerooms in May 1968, establishing a new world record price for paperweights. In the same category are the handsome snake weights, marred only by the trail of small air bubbles which baffled the craftsmen of Baccarat. Both lizards and snakes are usually shown on a ground simulating rocks, and a number of Baccarat weights are known with this rocky ground alone, the reptile for which they were designed being absent.

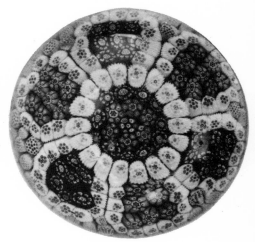

Among the miscellaneous weights which have been attributed to Baccarat may be mentioned the curious painted weights in which floral motifs have been painted on an opaque white ground. A very rare Baccarat weight is that which encloses the medal of the *Legion d'Honneur* instituted by Napoleon Bonaparte in 1802. These and other Bonapartist weights date from 1852–3 when Louis Napoleon (later Napoleon III) seized power. Two examples have been recorded of an unusual triple paperweight, consisting of three weights of different sizes which have been fused together. The tiny weight at the top contains an upright bouquet, the middle weight contains either scrambled or concentric millefiori while the large weight at the foot of the pyramid is a spaced millefiori on a muslin ground. This most curious of paperweights seems to have been confined to Baccarat.

The 'church' paperweight unearthed at Baccarat in 1951 contained 233 canes and was believed to be the work of Martin Kayser, Baccarat's master craftsman in the early 1850s. The discovery of this interesting weight stimulated the revival of millefiori paperweight manufacture at Baccarat, although, as has already been noted Dupont had worked in this field in the 1930s and Brocart had dabbled in it from 1947 onwards. Once the Baccarat factory returned to this field in earnest it took much longer to master the lost art than the original craftsmen had taken to imbibe the elements of the art from Venice and Bohemia. After six years of experiment and research Baccarat succeeded in producing a number of fine millefiori weights bearing the date 1957, or numbered

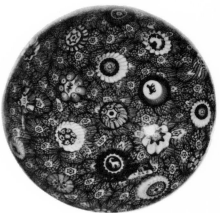

TOP Mushroom weight with close millefiori and a mercury ring. 3 in.

CENTRE Panelled carpet-ground with honeycomb canes, the panels outlined in white. 3⅛ in.

ABOVE A blue carpet-ground weight with silhouette canes and B1848 dated cane. 3¼ in.

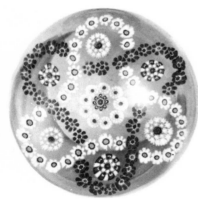

from 1 to 9. None of these experimental weights were marketed
commercially. The following year, however, a few weights were
distributed to retail outlets and bore a cane incised with the numeral
8 for identification purposes. Towards the end of 1958 further
identification was introduced in the form of silhouette canes bearing the signs of the Zodiac in black on white opaline. All Baccarat
millefiori weights produced since that time have included zodiac
silhouette canes, to defeat the possibility of unscrupulous dealers
passing off these modern weights as genuine Baccarat antiques.
In 1965, belatedly celebrating its bicentenary, Baccarat produced a
limited edition of millefiori paperweights containing one cane
bearing the inscription 'Baccarat 1764–1964' and individually
marked from A to Z. In addition to the 26 weights of this edition
there were 20 filigree weights with canes numbered from 1 to 20
and 20 crown weights numbered from 21 to 40. Most of these were
presented to Baccarat executives and employees and very few of
them have so far percolated through to the collectors' market.
Though the standard millefiori weights are not produced as a
limited edition the present Baccarat output is only about 300 weights
a year. Each paperweight contains from 180 to 220 canes (though
one contained as many as 245) and it takes three or four months to
build up a stock of canes sufficient to make 150 weights.

The crown, or *couronne* weights produced in recent years are, in
fact, small, simplified versions of the standard millefiori paperweights. Their canes, arranged in circles or *couronnes*, are not
pulled in the back of the weight all the way towards the centre as
in the true millefiori weights. They are just cut and laid flat, but
their pattern is often pretty none the less. Another modern paperweight, more sophisticated than the couronne, has cut canes lying
on a white latticinio ground and is known variously as the *semis de
perles* or filigree. This type of paperweight was revived by Baccarat
in 1958. Since then Baccarat have also experimented with more
elaborate filigree weights and with double overlays containing
bouquets. In a bid to get away from traditional paperweight
designs and perhaps emulating the work now being produced in
Scandinavia, Baccarat have introduced a range of paperweights in
clear crystal with simple geometric forms. These weights rejoice
under such names as 'Anchor', 'Star', 'Diamond', 'Maltese Cross',
'Cube' and 'Polygon', which are self-explanatory. Opaline weights
in a greyish blue opaque glass are also manufactured with either the
fleur-de-lys of Bourbon or the bees of the Napoleonic dynasty as
an overall motif in gold. The majority of modern weights from
this factory have the inscription 'Baccarat France' etched within a
small circle on the base.

Seven

St Louis Paperweights

The history and output of St Louis is strangely parallel to that of Baccarat. A glassworks was established in the village of St Louis, near Bitche in Lorraine, in 1767, barely three years after the foundation of the Baccarat factory and less than a year after the Duchy of Lorraine lost its independence to France. The *Verrerie Royale de St Louis*, as its name implied, enjoyed royal patronage and rapidly attained a technical excellence on a par with the best English and Venetian glass. In the Revolution and its aftermath the glasshouse endured numerous vicissitudes but recovered in the early nineteenth century and changed its name in 1829 to the *Compagnie des Cristalleries de St Louis*. By the late 1830s the factory was specialising in coloured glassware and began producing paperweights in the early 1840s. In 1832 St Louis joined forces with Baccarat to purchase the rival Creusot glasshouse. From then onwards these two firms were the largest and most important in the French glass industry, a position which they hold to this day. After 1871, when Lorraine was ceded to the German Empire, the company continued to function, though the production of paperweights is thought to have come to a halt some time before that date. Significantly no mention is made of St Louis in the glass exhibits of the 1878 *Exposition Universelle*, though both Baccarat and Clichy are mentioned in some detail. Lorraine returned to France under the terms of the Treaty of Versailles in 1919 and apart from the brief period from 1940 to 1944 when it was incorporated in the Third Reich, Lorraine has remained French ever since. The turbulent politics of the past century inevitably had their repercussions on the fortunes of the St Louis glassworks, but today it has recovered its former eminence and has also begun to take part, to a limited extent, in the revival of interest in paperweight production.

The classic paperweights of St Louis were much higher domed than those from Baccarat and were made of very clear, heavy lead glass. Like Baccarat, St Louis favoured a star cut base, especially for bouquet and mushroom weights. Relatively few St Louis weights included dated canes, these dates being confined to the years from 1845 to 1849, with 1848 being the date most commonly encountered. The numerals may be found in blue, purple, mauve or red, often in conjunction with the initials SL in black or blue letters. These initials may also be found in undated weights. Compared with Baccarat and Clichy St Louis had a fairly limited range

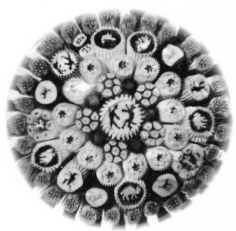

TOP Four-colour crown weight. 3 in.

ABOVE An extremely rare 'Double Devil' weight with a spiral latticinio cushion. 3⅛ in.

43

Close millefiori weight
with blue and white
spirals at the base.
3¼ in.

BELOW Very rare
upright bouquet with
'oranges and lemons'
base and concave
printies. 3¼ in.

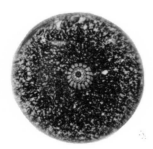

Miniature jasper-
ground weight. 1¾ in.

of cane types and as these are quite distinctive identification is usually simple. Apart from the usual stars and cogs there is a distinctive six-petalled blossom, a circle in a sunburst, an anchor device (not unlike the Baccarat arrowhead, but with a rounded point), a circle containing a group of nine small circles arranged in a square pattern and a catherine wheel.

The silhouette canes form an interesting and varied group, though they are generally less realistic than those of Baccarat. The animals and birds include a camel, a turkey, a dog of indeterminate breed and a duck with its duckling. The human figures include two different types of dancing girl, a dancing faun and a dancing couple. There was also the ubiquitous devil and a curious figure which defies description, since it looks like a clown or an anteater, depending which way up it is viewed! A portrait cane, which is really a miniature sulphide profile, has been tentatively identified as Pauline Borghese. The monotony and irregularity of the mille-fiori patterns in St Louis weights is balanced by the striking colours and attractive combinations which this glasshouse devised.

The earliest St Louis weights were of the close millefiori pattern and bore a striking resemblance to the early Bohemian weights, in that the canes fill almost the whole of the globe and come quite close to the surface. Since very few of these weights are dated 1845, it is presumed that the majority of them were in fact produced earlier than that year. Technically these close millefiori weights lack the polish and competence of subsequent weights, the canes being often carelessly arranged. Somewhat later than these are the scattered or scrambled millefiori weights, a few of which are packed close to the summit of the dome, though more often they are set lower down and use is made of the magnifying properties of the glass. Pieces of latticinio and stripes of coloured glass are often mixed up with the millefiori canes in a glorious hotch-potch of colour. These weights were among the earliest produced at St Louis. As the craftsmen became more proficient in this medium the patterned paperweights began to appear. These include the cross pattern, in which the four segments of close millefiori are separated from each other by a cross composed of uniform mille-fiori canes. St Louis produced a few patterned weights with the millefiori arranged in a heart or a circle. Concentric patterns are relatively common and these are among the finest weights ever produced by this firm.

A speciality of the St Louis factory was its so-called 'jasper ground' composed of partially pulverised glass, which formed the basis for some of the most attractive flower weights. A variant of this was the jasper panelled weight in which contrasting panels of

Camomile on a
swirling pink and white
latticinio ground.
$2\frac{5}{8}$ in.

FAR LEFT A dahlia
weight, the large
flower filling the
weight close to the
surface. $2\frac{1}{2}$ in.

LEFT Miniature blue
dahlia weight. $1\frac{3}{4}$ in.

ABOVE Fuchsia weight
on a latticinio ground.
3 in.

Red-petalled flower
weight on a clear
ground. $2\frac{1}{2}$ in.

jasper and green were separated by thick white spokes. The centre,
or axle of the wheel, might contain a single sihouette cane or a small
turban swirl, while millefiori canes were often set between the
spokes close to the hub. Very few of the coloured ground weights
produced at St Louis were decorated with garlands or nosegays of
millefiori, but the few examples which have been identified are
usually in the shape of a six-pointed star, made up of uniform
groups of millefiori canes. Carpet grounds, somewhat similar to
those of Baccarat, may be distinguished by their predilection for
crimped canes and the predominantly pink or green overall effect.
The uniform effect of these carpet grounds is occasionally relieved
by a few spaced millefiori florets or silhouette canes. The St Louis
carpet weights were usually large (at least three inches in diameter)
and are among the most impressive of all the classic weights.

St Louis produced some beautiful mushroom weights, with
relatively small tufts crammed with millefiori, and a surrounding
torsade composed of latticinio or spirals of white opaque threads.
This glasshouse also produced a few crown weights, the only
French factory to emulate this Venetian type of paperweight. 45

TOP Unripe raspberry
weight in clear glass.
2⅜ in.

ABOVE Red-currant
weight in clear
glass. 2¾ in.

A faceted cherry
weight. 2½ in.

These weights consist of hollow, slightly flattened globes whose walls are lined with white filigree twists alternating with twisted coloured ribbons of glass, usually joined at the top by a single millefiori cane. On their base there is usually a hole where the glass-blower's iron has been withdrawn. Though not made by any of the other French factories in the classic period it is interesting to note that the crown weight was imitated by the American glasshouses and is one of the forms which the modern Baccarat programme has revived.

There are several different kinds of flower weight attributed to St Louis. The flat bouquet consisted of several millefiori blossoms grouped together, with leaves and stems, on a jasper or coloured ground and having a circular border of millefiori canes. There are many variations on this theme, with different grounds, concentric millefiori rings and arrangements of the bouquet itself. Most of these weights are regular in shape, but a few are faceted all over in a style distinctive to St Louis. A few bouquets are known with an attractive torsade surround in delicate colours.

Distinctive flower weights from this factory include the ubiquitous pansy, clematis, camomile, geranium (sometimes described as anemone), fuchsia, dahlia and a very rare flower which cannot be identified as any particular species but approximates to the chrysanthemum. These individual flowers may be found on a jasper ground or, more often, a latticinio swirl of white or pink opaque glass. Fruit weights assigned to St Louis include strawberries, cherries and grapes as well as a basket arrangement containing a group of small fruits (pears and cherries). Again, a latticinio ground was commonly employed. Other fruit weights, featuring currants, grapes, pears and apples, may or may not have emanated from St Louis, and Pantin is sometimes given credit for these weights. All of them are scarce and though technically well done lack the appeal of the flower weights.

St Louis specialised in various kinds of overlay weights, including double overlays and encased overlays in which one or more overlays have been applied in coloured glass and then a heavy coating of clear crystal glass applied to encase the weight. The cutting of the printies was always carried out with great care and precision. There is even a triple overlay, with royal blue over opaque white, now preserved in the Corning Museum of Glass. Multi-faceted weights and hand coolers containing upright bouquets were another St Louis speciality. Among the rarest of all St Louis weights are the curious 'marbrie' weights. These unusual weights are hollow and derive their name from the French word for marble (*Marbre*), though the appearance of the marbrie weights is not akin to marble.

A very rare grapevine
weight with 7 windows
on top and 6 in the
sides, strawberry cut.
2½ in.

A vegetable weight
with five turnips in a
basket of swirling
latticinio. 2⅞ in.

A rare strawberry
weight with two fruit
and three leaves on a
clear ground. It is very
rare for it either not to
have a white flower or
be on a latticinio
ground. 2⅞ in.

Mixed fruit weight on a
latticinio panel and
clear surround. 3¼ in.

Pelargonium weight on
a latticinio ground.
3 in.

A rare pansy weight in
clear glass with a
diamond-cut base.
3¼ in.

A very rare encased
blue and white overlay
weight with an upright
central posy, 2
silhouettes of horses in
opaque panels on the
sides and a circular
window on top. 3⅛ in.

These weights contain a single white opaque overlay festooned with trailed swags of blue, red, green or some other bright colour, with a single millefiori cane or floret at the apex. St Louis produced comparatively few weights featuring insects, birds or animals and as a class they are so rare as to be represented by a handful of items. A single frog weight has been attributed to St Louis, a few attractive lizards and snakes and some sulphide overlays containing a fish which has been identified as carp, a unique retriever dog weight and some curious long-legged 'parrots' comprise the St Louis menagerie. A few others, including a unique squirrel and a grasshopper weight, have sometimes been attributed to St Louis, though some authorities think that they may have originated at Pantin.

The classic paperweights of St Louis were almost all produced within the span of six years. The company did not take part in the Great Exhibition of 1851 and in reports of its glassware displayed at subsequent exhibitions paperweights are conspicuous by their absence. Unlike Baccarat, St Louis seems to have abandoned paperweights completely from 1850 onwards. A century later, however, St Louis half-heartedly revived an interest in paperweight production. Like Baccarat they produced a sulphide weight to mark the coronation of Queen Elizabeth and then went on to make a number of concentric millefiori weights, as well as a range of flower, fruit and vegetable weights, some featuring a dragonfly and a number of related items such as shot cups and vases with a heavy millefiori base. These weights were surprisingly well executed, considering that a century of inactivity had intervened since St Louis last essayed paperweight production. St Louis lagged behind Baccarat in the resumption of paperweight manufacture on a large scale. A few were produced in the early 1960s but then production lapsed until 1969 when limited editions of millefiori and flower weights were released. These modern weights are superlative in quality and are well up to the technical standards of the classic weights. Many, though not all, modern St Louis weights bear the date and the initials SL. The old predeliction for multi-facetting has been revived with a vengeance and some of the mid-1960s examples are elaborately facetted over their entire surface.

The commercial limited editions started in 1969. Three types were produced: 1,000 mushroom overlays, 800 dahlias and 800 red or yellow flowers on a purple ground. These weights contained a central floret with the date below the initials SL. Similar editions appeared in 1970 and, at the time of writing (mid-1972) are still available in Britain and Europe. No subsequent dates have yet been seen. These weights are very expensive (£75–£100) and the prices are comparable to the commoner weights of the classic period.

Eight

Clichy Paperweights

The third French glasshouse to specialise in paperweights had only been established for a few years when these attractive baubles became fashionable. Joseph Maes founded a glassworks at Billancourt (Sèvres) in 1837 and about two years later moved to Clichy-la-Garenne on the outskirts of Paris. Initially the company concentrated on cheap lines for export but in the early 1840s began to develop more expensive wares of a very high quality, so that by the time of the 1844 *Exposition* the glass of Clichy was being compared most favourably with that of Baccarat and St Louis. These two old-established firms declined to participate in the Great Exhibition of 1851 and Clichy walked off with the main prize in the glassmaking section. Under the direction of Maes and his partner Clemandot Clichy prospered, as the prizes which it won in international exhibitions in the 1850s and 1860s indicate. When St Louis dropped out of paperweight production about 1850 Clichy stepped in and filled the orders which their competitors were either unable or unwilling to deal with.

In 1853 Clichy took part in the Crystal Palace Exhibition staged in New York and Horace Greeley's comments on the products of the company, printed in a lengthy article in the *New York Tribune*, are worth quoting: "The collection of Mr. Maez (*sic*) of Clichy, near Paris, is a very extensive and beautiful one. Besides being a manufacturer of glass, he is also well acquainted with the chemical department of his art, as is evinced by the beauty and novelty of some of his productions, for which he has received two medals; from his own country and from England at the London Exhibition. The latter was given for lenses and glass for optical instruments; a Council medal for novelty of chemical application, and a prize medal for a prism of zinc glass. Not only is the ornamentation and coloring of Mr. Maez's collection of great merit, but in the design and form of the vessels there is great taste. The paperweights are here in innumerable variety."

Clichy was the sole French firm to take part in the glass section of the Great Exhibition of 1862 in London and subsequently the company participated in the French *Expositions* of 1867 and 1878. Some paperweights were still being produced in the late 1860s, but by the time of the 1878 exhibition "this establishment was living off its past glory", as the jury of 1878 put it unkindly in their report. The quality of Clichy glass deteriorated rapidly after the Franco-Prussian War. In 1885 the business founded by Maes was pur-

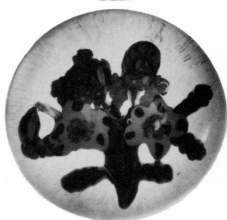

TOP A small cornucopia weight on a clear ground. 2¾ in.

ABOVE A rare strawberry and flower, flat bouquet weight in clear glass. 2⅜ in.

LEFT Rare initial medallion weight with monogram AH in blue over white staves. 3¾ in.

RIGHT Faceted mushroom weight with an outer basket of turquoise and white staves. 3 in.

BELOW LEFT An unusual pink rose weight on an opaque white ground. 2¼ × 2⅛ in.

chased by the Lander family who operated a glasshouse at Sèvres. The company was renamed *Cristalleries de Sèvres et Clichy*, but despite the retention of the old name the products of this company were well below the standard associated with Clichy and henceforward it dropped into merciful oblivion.

The period in which Clichy paperweights was produced cannot be ascertained with accuracy, since it was not the company's practice to date their weights. It seems probable that they were being made in 1846 or late 1845 and continued rather longer than Baccarat, with sporadic production up to about 1870. The heyday of the Clichy paperweight was the period from 1846 to 1852. In profile

LEFT Triple-colour swirl weight, the ribbons in white, purple and green. 3¼ in.

BELOW Blue and white swirl weight with a pink centre.

A fine dark-blue overlay basket weight with white and mauve staves. 2¾ in.

Clichy weights resemble a perfect globular form terminated somewhat abruptly by a flat base. Though not generally as high-domed as those of St Louis they exhibited a more perfectly rounded appearance. The base was very slightly concave with a very narrow, flat rim. Most Clichy weights have a slightly depressed ring near the base, usually coinciding with the edge of the ground and suggesting a mould mark not entirely removed in the subsequent working of the glass. The glass is clear and generally lighter than that of Baccarat or St Louis. Overlay weights have a decorative pattern on their base, either star cut or strawberry cut, and sometimes cut in tiny squares resembling graph paper. This feature was distinctive to Clichy and was a sure method of identification until recently when Muranese glasshouses began to imitate Clichy classic weights to deceive collectors.

Much has been made, by previous writers on the subject, of the famous Clichy rose, a millefiori cane which is found in about a third of all Clichy paperweights. While rose canes were by no means the monopoly of Clichy the floret used by this company was quite distinctive. It was very small and consisted of a bundle of tiny rods surrounded by flattened tubes to form the petals. There were several varieties of the Clichy rose, with either circular or cross-shaped pattern or occasionally a whorl device in the centre. These rose canes are found in an enormous variety of shades and colours.

Clichy used an assortment of canes which was the equal of Baccarat in its range, but certain forms predominate. They include the distinctive 'pastry-mould' canes which may easily be recognised by their deeply ruffled skirt. Another readily recognisable type is the Clichy whorl, composed of fine concentric circles. There was also the usual range of crimped tubes, star canes and cog-wheels, but square patterned canes were rarely used. A few Clichy weights contain an opaque white cane with the letter C in black, blue, red or green. The letter is always heavily seriffed so that it is sometimes mistaken for a horseshoe. A very few weights have the name inscribed in full. Silhouette canes are unknown in Clichy paperweights, an eliminating factor which should be borne in mind when attempting to identify weights.

Though Clichy weights were not dated there is a unique exception, produced in connection with the Great Exhibition of 1851. The base was incised with a crowned monogram VA (for Victoria and Albert) and beneath it 'Londres, 1851'. This unique example passed through Sotheby's saleroom in 1955 and is now in the Corning Museum of Glass, New York. The weight itself, though contained in a special leather case, is only an average specimen of Clichy workmanship, a large-spaced millefiori weight in clear glass.

A rare rose weight on clear glass with air bubbles round the flower and bud. 3 in.

Triple flower weight, depicting a rose and two clematis tied with ribbon. 2¾ in.

A rare daisy weight in clear glass. 2⅝ in.

A fine flower weight in clear glass. 3 in.

51

A pansy weight in clear glass. 3 in.

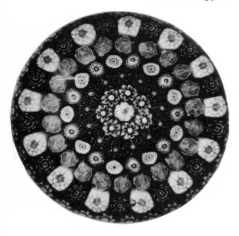

Concentric millefiori weight in a basket of white staves. 3¼ in.

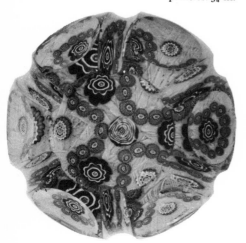

A faceted weight on an upset muslin ground with a trefoil garland and fluted printies. 3¼ in.

Clichy went through the entire gamut of paperweight types, though each has its distinctive characteristics which make identification fairly straightforward. The scrambled millefiori weights which this company produced in great profusion and in all sizes, have a predominantly green overall pattern, though canes of many other colours were intermingled. Spaced millefiori weights come in two distinct forms, one which creates the illusion of being scattered, on account of the uneven size and spacing of the canes towards the edge of the circumference, and the so-called 'chequer' weights in which the canes were separated by fine latticinio. The 'scattered' spaced millefiori weights are generally mounted on opaque, translucent or muslin grounds. Close millefiori weights were seldom produced by this factory, though it is in these weights that the Clichy rose in its many guises is most often to be found.

Clichy produced a wide range of millefiori weights with concentric patterns, with as many as eight circles of canes in a tightly packed formation on a clear glass ground. Others, with three or four rings, are on coloured or muslin grounds. The Clichy coloured grounds usually consisted of an opaque white base with a translucent overlay of rich ruby and shades of red, or shades of blue ranging from deep cobalt to sky blue, or shades of green from pale lime to vivid emerald. These coloured grounds are seen at their best in the attractive garland weights which were a Clichy speciality. Clichy devised an enormous variety of garland patterns with combinations of loops and circles so that scarcely two will be found that are alike. Other patterns favoured by Clichy were stars and C-scrolls, in which the canes were arranged in concentric stars or in groups of four or five semi-circles resembling a large capital C, with concentric circles in the centre.

The Clichy rose is also found in swirl paperweights, with contrasting bands of opaque white and pink or purple stripes. Clichy also made weights in which the bands radiating from the central rose were straight, like the spokes of a wheel, rather than curving at their extremeties in the usual swirl pattern.

Clichy made very few bouquet weights, with a group of three or four florets on a clear or muslin ground and sometimes surrounded by a border of millefiori canes. Other weights show a group of flowers laid haphazardly on a latticinio ground as though they had just been picked. Clichy made the usual pansy weights, in great profusion and variety, but also produced a few weights containing other kinds of flowers, some of which cannot be identified as any particular species and others which have been named as morning glory or convolvulus, mignonette or scabiosa. These flat floral weights from Clichy are of great beauty and rarity. There is some

A circle of roses on a
dark-blue ground.
$2\frac{5}{8}$ in.

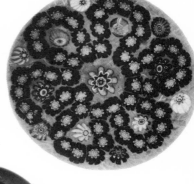

A rare colour ground
chequer weight. $3\frac{1}{4}$ in.

Interlaced garlands
weight on a purple
ground. $3\frac{1}{4}$ in.

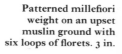

Patterned millefiori
weight on an upset
muslin ground with
six loops of florets. 3 in.

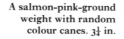

A salmon-pink-ground
weight with random
colour canes. $3\frac{1}{4}$ in.

A typical 'barber's
pole' weight, the
muslin ground divided
by red and white
twisted ribbons. $3\frac{1}{4}$ in.

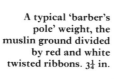

53

TOP A weight with loops of pastry-mould canes on an apple-green ground. 3½ in.

CENTRE A single flower weight on a moss ground. 3 in.

ABOVE An attractive patterned millefiori weight with 4 entwined garlands. 3¼ in.

doubt as to whether Clichy ever made fruit weights, but one featuring two strawberries has been tentatively ascribed to this glasshouse.

A single basket paperweight has been discovered and attributed to Clichy. It is in the shape of a basket, with vertical white staves and red and white twist ribbons marking the top and bottom perimeters. The sides are slightly nipped in and there are marks indicating that a glass handle had originally been fitted to the top of the basket. The contents of the basket consist of concentric millefiori with clusters of florets about the outer perimeter. A very thin covering of clear glass preserves the illusion of the basket of flowers rather than a traditional paperweight. A few close or concentric millefiori weights were mounted on a pedestal surrounded by staves of opaque white glass. These weights are sometimes known as 'pedouche' weights.

Though Clichy did not make the same extensive use of facetting found in St Louis or Baccarat, it produced some unusual examples in which vertical fluting was ground between the printies. Hollister also records a probably unique example of a white overlay weight cut in melon-rib style with ten deep vertical flutes running from the base to the apex of the weight with a single Clichy rose set at the top. Inside is a low-ground, close millefiori pattern which can only be glimpsed through the narrow fluting. Clichy made a few overlay weights with printies cut in the overlays. The majority of these overlay weights are doubles with an inner overlay of white and an outer overlay in shades of red, green or blue. The printies are comparatively large and slightly concave, with a single large flat printy cut into the top of the dome. The interior of such overlay weights is usually a close or concentric millefiori pattern in a basket with white staves.

Apart from paperweights Clichy manufactured a few objects incorporating millefiori patterns. These included globular mounts for newel posts and bed posts, inkwells and perfume bottles, decanters and door-knobs. The millefiori was contained in clear glass in either the base or the stopper. A pair of vases with an overall millefiori pattern has also been attributed to Clichy.

Within recent years the *Cristalleries de Sèvres* have produced attractive glass paperweights which depart from the millefiori tradition of the classic Clichy weights. These are in moulded glass with a high lead content and usually take the form of animals and birds on a fairly solid, broad base. An attractive weight from this factory consists of a polar bear in frosted glass mounted on a solid sloping cylinder of clear glass. These weights and other glass novelties from this factory have the name 'Sèvres' etched lightly on the base.

A pebble-ground weight containing a silhouette cane of the devil. (SPINK & SON)

BELOW A flat bouquet weight on a clear ground. (TILLMAN)

ST LOUIS

LEFT A rare floral overlay weight. (SPINK & SON)

BELOW A mixed fruit weight on a latticinio ground. (SPINK & SON)

ST LOUIS

An exceptionally rare salamander, the black and gold reptile lies on a blue ground. (SPINK & SON)

A fine three-coloured marbrie weight. (TILLMAN)

RIGHT A large flat bouquet weight on a clear ground. (TILLMAN)

A close millefiori weight. (SPINK & SON)

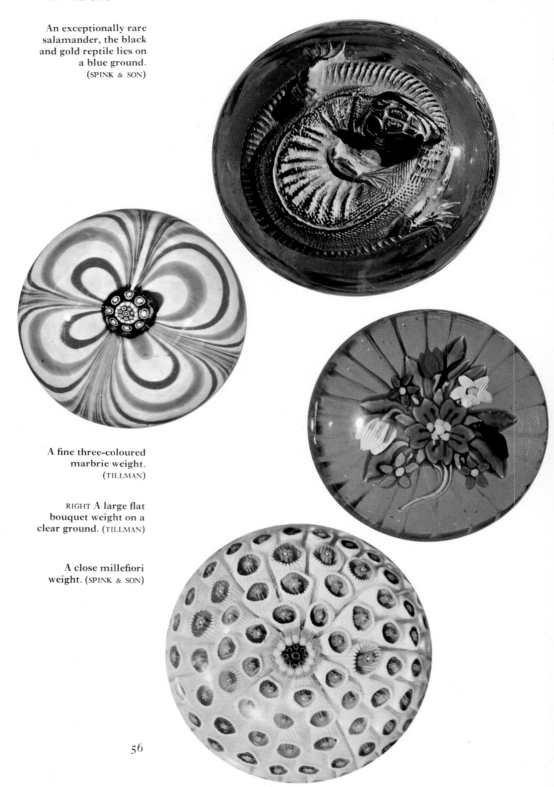

56

CLICHY

A millefiori garland on a deep purple ground. (SPINK & SON)

LEFT An attractive bouquet weight on a clear ground. (SPINK & SON)

FAR LEFT A characteristic C-shaped garland weight on a sky-blue ground. (SPINK & SON)

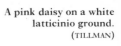

A pink daisy on a white latticinio ground. (TILLMAN)

57

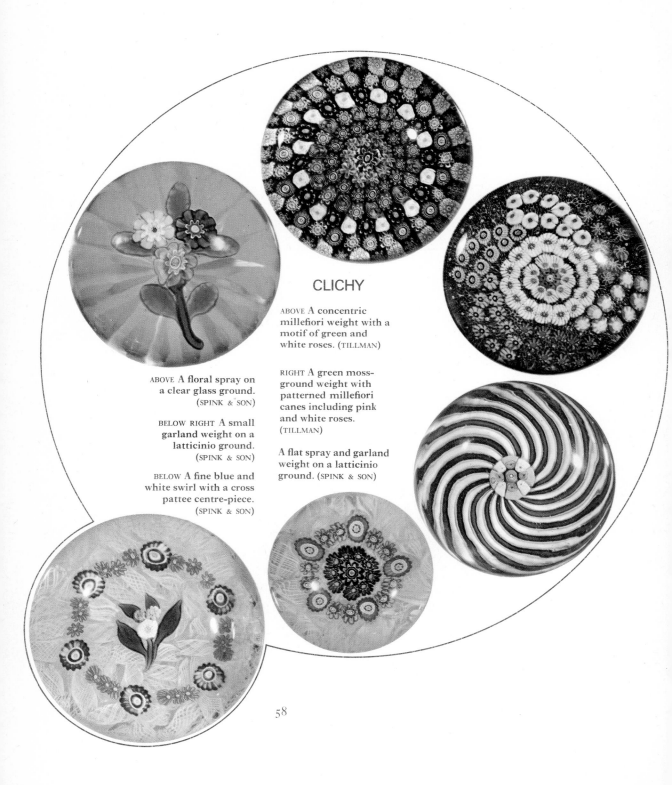

CLICHY

ABOVE A concentric millefiori weight with a motif of green and white roses. (TILLMAN)

RIGHT A green moss-ground weight with patterned millefiori canes including pink and white roses. (TILLMAN)

A flat spray and garland weight on a latticinio ground. (SPINK & SON)

ABOVE A floral spray on a clear glass ground. (SPINK & SON)

BELOW RIGHT A small garland weight on a latticinio ground. (SPINK & SON)

BELOW A fine blue and white swirl with a cross pattee centre-piece. (SPINK & SON)

Nine

English Paperweights

The inventiveness of the English, who produced the splendid lead glass of the late seventeenth century, was stifled by the stupidity of successive governments who imposed heavy duties on glass from 1745 onwards. Hampered by the iniquitous Glass Excise the English manufacturers looked on helplessly while their competitors in Venice, Bohemia and France cornered the market and many were forced to transfer their production to Ireland where the hated tax did not apply. At the end of the Napoleonic Wars the tax stood at $10\frac{1}{2}$d (4p) per pound weight of glass, a prohibitive impost which all but killed the industry. In 1825 the tax was lowered to 6d ($2\frac{1}{2}$p) per pound but not abolished until 1845, the very year in which glass paperweights burst so dramatically on the scene.

The removal of the Glass Excise permitted a fantastic revival in the manufacture of glass, in quantity, quality and diversity. Appropriately the venue of the Great Exhibition staged six years later was the gigantic Crystal Palace built of almost a million square feet of plate glass, a triumphant demonstration of the recovery of the industry in England. The range and quality of the glassware displayed at this exhibition was phenomenal and inevitably paperweights formed part of the range. The majority of English paperweights were millefiori and derived their inspiration from the great French manufacturers. This is understandable, since the English glasshouses were striving to produce an article which was popular with the public and for which the market, though recent, was already well established. Nevertheless the English companies experimented with glass paperweights of types never found in France and indeed, from the work of Pellatt and others in the preceding decade, it can be seen that the English had their own valuable contribution to make to the art of the paperweight.

Because English paperweights of the classic period were comparatively neglected until recently, research into their antecedents was never so painstaking nor so far-reaching as that conducted into the French firms. Consequently many misconceptions have arisen and are only now being laid to rest.

The most persistent of these misconceptions is that glass paperweights were made at Bristol and neighbouring Nailsea in the nineteenth century. In the eighteenth century both towns were the centre of a glassmaking industry which specialised in coloured glass, particularly the famous Bristol blue glass, but by the 1840s, when paperweights came into popularity, glassmaking was dying 59 out in the west country. The millefiori weights containing an initial B cane are now known to have been produced in Venice (Bigaglia) or Baccarat and include those produced by Dupont for Baccarat in the early 1930s. The possibility of paperweights having been made in Bristol cannot be entirely ruled out, but industrial archaeologists have so far failed to unearth any practical evidence from an examination of the old factory sites. Nailsea has often been credited with the manufacture of the large bottle-green weights which are still quite plentiful in England but these weights, discussed later in this chapter, were produced by Kilner and other glassmakers mainly in the Yorkshire area.

The other great myth concerning English paperweights is that they were produced in the Stourbridge area of the west Midlands. Stourbridge was, and still is, an important centre of the glass industry, specialising not only in plate and industrial glass but contributing a great deal to the development of art and fancy glass in the nineteenth century. Yet apart from a few oral traditions asserting that paperweights were made in that district no positive evidence has been produced to support this claim, and many of the weights which have hitherto been ascribed to Stourbridge have now been proved to have come from Birmingham or London. Here again, however, the possibility of paperweight production cannot be ruled out entirely and there are still several weights whose provenance has not been established and which, for the sake of convenience as much as anything, dealers and auctioneers continue to label as Stourbridge.

Early 19th century door-stop weight, double flower and pot in green glass. 5 in. high.

WHITEFRIARS

The principal manufacturer of paperweights in England, then as now, is the Whitefriars company of London. A glassworks was in existence on the site of the old monastery of the White Friars in the last quarter of the seventeenth century and produced flint glass for domestic purposes. The company was rejuvenated in 1835 when James Powell, a Bristol glassmaker, took it over and renamed it James Powell & Sons. Under new management the company rose to pre-eminence in England, its products ranging from humble domestic wares to telescope lenses and stained glass for church windows. The company was awarded a medal at the Great Exhibition of 1851 for its fine crystal glass, which also drew from Eugéne Pèligot a favourable comment in his report made on behalf of the French Commissioners for the Exhibition. There was no mention of paperweights, though Powells had been producing them for at least three years. For much of the nineteenth century Whitefriars clung to conventional products, but under the direction of Harry J. Powell (1853–1922) the company began, at the turn of the century, to revive glassmaking as an art and since then has been in the fore-front of the production of hand-blown glass, fine hand-engraved vases and goblets and art glass of a superlative quality. In this revival paperweights have played an intermittent part and although their production is not conducted with the singlemindedness which is the current Baccarat hallmark, Whitefriars have turned out some excellent work in this field over the past twenty years. In the 1920s the firm moved out of London to Wealdstone in Middlesex where it continued to be known as James Powell & Sons (Whitefriars) Ltd, until recently when the name was simplified to Whitefriars Glass Ltd. Its products bear the stylised emblem of a White Friar which sometimes resembles a lower-case 'i' or a candle in white against a dark blue background.

A spiral door-stop weight with a flower and spiral bubble motif.

The production of paperweights by this company is tantalisingly obscure. Until recently it was never conducted as a serious or deliberate part of the company's operations but seems always to have been regarded as a sideline. It is generally accepted that mille-fiori paperweights were first produced at Whitefriars in 1848 and that their manufacture has been continuous since that date, with surprisingly little variation in the distinctive profiles adopted. Three characteristic types were produced – a very shallow weight with a flat base, a higher-domed type not unlike that favoured by the French glasshouses, and an unusual type with a very high dome, straight sides and a footed rim. Whitefriars produced millefiori weights in either close or concentric patterns. So far as can be ascertained this firm never attempted to make garlands or scattered millefiori weights, nor ventured into the realm of flower, fruit and insect weights. Whitefriars also manufactured wine glasses, de-canters, goblets and inkwells with millefiori bases or stoppers. Again very little is known about them or the period in which they were produced.

One cannot speak of a clearcut revival at Whitefriars, as happened in the case of Baccarat and St Louis, since the production of paper-weights has been sporadically conducted over the past 120 years, but it is significant that the coronation of Queen Elizabeth in 1953 was the occasion of the first commercial paperweight deliberately marketed by Whitefriars. Between 600 and 700 concentric paper-weights with a central cane inscribed 'E II R 1953' were made to celebrate the event and are now highly prized as collector's pieces or Coronation souvenirs. Despite the success of this weight White-friars did not take up paperweight production on a large scale again until 1965 when some 400 weights were marketed. Even since that date production seems to have gone in fits and starts.

The earliest Whitefriars weights were of the very shallow type   61 described above. Despite their low dome these weights made use of the magnifying properties of the surrounding glass. An interesting feature of these and many other Whitefriars paperweights is the appearance of the base which indicates quite clearly the inner circle on which the millefiori canes are assembled, and the outer casing of the clear glass dome. The bottoms of the canes come very close to the base. A few examples have been recorded in which the original manufacturer's label is still intact and this shows a white-robed friar holding a board inscribed WHITEFRIARS, with POWELLS ENGLISH GLASS round the edge. Modern paperweights, unlike other Whitefriars products, are sold without the stylised white friar emblem on a label, but its absence is usually compensated for by the inclusion of a cane bearing the white friar motif.

Relatively few different types of cane have been used by White-friars over the years and these consist basically of single rods or tubes enclosing single rods. Crimps, cogs, stars, trefoils and quatrefoils are the types of cane favoured by Whitefriars. What they lose in their limited form is made up for in the pleasing range of colours in a multitude of permutations and combinations. Super-ficially Whitefriars weights may seem blue, purple, green or red, but a closer examination will reveal that all colours of the spectrum are represented. Just before the Second World War Whitefriars began to include more interesting canes in their weights and related millefiori objects. These canes include playing card motifs such as spades and diamonds and more exotic motifs composed of a trefoil with four spots surrounding it. Whitefriars weights are undated, with the exception of a few produced in 1848, with the digits on separate white canes, and the coronation paperweights already referred to. Modern weights contain a cane with the white friar emblem in white on a dark blue background. Some of the most

A glass incrustation by Apsley Pellatt commemorating the laying of the foundation stone of the Royal Exchange by Prince Albert in January 1842.

recent weights have a two-tone blue cane with the emblem in the centre and the date in four tiny rods in the lower segment of the circle.

The early paperweights included a good number of close mille-fiori patterns in which the canes were packed close together in every colour of the rainbow. This type of close millefiori pattern was also used for inkwells, perfume bottles and decanters. The majority of Whitefriars weights follow a concentric pattern with the circles very close set and anything up to ten circles surrounding a central star cane. In some of these weights the canes are virtually identical, but in others there is an attractive contrast in the colours and shapes of the circles of canes. Indeed, in the matter of harmonious combinations of colour and form, the best of the Whitefriars weights would be hard to beat. Whitefriars also produced a few chequer weights of academic rather than aesthetic interest. The technique of spacing the latticinio between the clusters of millefiori defeated the White-friars craftsmen and the majority of these chequer weights present a hopeless jumble. Whitefriars did not persevere with this de-ceptively difficult technique and such weights are therefore com-paratively rare. Only one attempt at an overlay weight has been attributed to Whitefriars, a curious white overlay with blue stripes on its inner surface. Through the printies can be seen an attractive concentric pattern of blue, orange and red canes. In recent years Whitefriars have manufactured concentrics with printies cut in their sides and top.

BACCHUS

Birmingham in the early nineteenth century was an important glassmaking centre. Among the firms then in operation was Bacchus, Green and Green of the Union Glass Works. The name of the company changed in 1833 to George Bacchus & Co, Bacchus being in partnership with George Joseph Green and William Gammon, the latter having formerly operated his own factory. In 1840 George Bacchus died and his son, John Bacchus took control. The following year the company changed its name to George Bacchus & Sons and contracted it to Bacchus & Sons in 1858. Two years later the firm was absorbed by Stone, Fawdry & Stone.

Bacchus originally produced domestic glassware and plate glass but after 1845 began experimenting with fancy glass in the Vene-tian manner and by 1848 had also produced paperweights. The *Art Union Monthly Journal of the Arts* (1849) had this interesting comment under the heading Glass Paper Weights: "The intro-duction of these ingenious and pretty ornaments from Bohemia has induced some of our glass manufacturers to turn their attention

So-called Stourbridge millefiori inkwell and stopper. 5½ in. high.

to the production of similar objects. We have seen a large number of home manufacture, which, for beauty and variety of colour, are equal to the best imported; and in design are superior to them. Mr. Bacchus, an eminent glass manufacturer of Birmingham, has produced some that deserve special notice for their novelty and elegance."

In that year Bacchus took part in the Exhibition of Manufactures and Art in Birmingham and among the assortment of more than 100 different articles were displayed "letter weights". Though these items were only a sideline to the company's main operations they caught the attention of discerning contemporary writers. The *Journal of Design and Manufactures* (1849), commenting on Bacchus paperweights, stated "the specimens we have recently seen of their works are quite the equal in transparency, colour, skillful arrangement of parts and ingenuity of make, to the foreign works with which stationers' and fancy shops have been and are so crowded."

Two years later Bacchus won a medal at the Great Exhibition for their glass, though no mention appears in the list of paperweights. Too little is known of this factory in general or its products in particular to state positively when paperweights ceased to be produced but it seems likely that this aspect of the company's business had declined rapidly after 1850. Perhaps the products of Baccarat, St Louis and Clichy were too well entrenched by that date for Bacchus to compete with them profitably. At any rate it is thought that no more than four hundred weights were manufactured by Bacchus. They are now so scarce that even in their home country no more than a handful pass through the salerooms in the course of a year. No doubt there are homes in England, especially in Birmingham and the Midlands, where Bacchus weights repose unconsidered and unknown, for remarkably little reference has ever been made to this firm in the literature of paperweights.

The great majority of Bacchus weights are large in size and are usually over three inches in diameter. In profile they are not particularly high-domed but have a pronounced curve in their sides, terminating in a base considerably less in diameter than the weight at its greatest girth. A characteristic feature of Bacchus weights is the comparatively high cushion on which the canes are set. This has the appearance of being undercut so that the canes at the edge are drawn under sharply, almost to the centre of the base. Bacchus relied on four basic types of cane, a six-pointed star in a circle, the ruffle composed of concentric six-pointed stars superimposed on a six-pointed cross, a straightforward crimped cane and a cog which sometimes resembles a sunburst. Variety was attained, however, by the adroit use of colour and, above all, of size, for the rods which comprised these canes ranged from microscopic to quite large dimensions. There were also intriguing combinations of different canes to make up a large composite cane. An exceedingly diffuse range of colours was employed, with shades of green, red, purple and blue predominating. A silhouette cane of a woman's profile is occasionally encountered in Bacchus weights. No dated canes have been recorded for this company and though Baccarat weights with the initial B have sometimes been wrongly attributed to Bacchus, no weights have been found with an identifying letter or inscription.

Bacchus produced a few close millefiori weights, distinguished by relatively large canes and the characteristic way in which the outer ring of canes is cupped underneath almost to the centre of the base. The vast majority of the Bacchus weights, however, were concentrics, and again the curious cupping of the outer ring to the centre of the base underneath is a Bacchus hallmark. The concentric weights have, on average, five circles of canes, one or more of which is composed of fairly large canes. In the centre there is either a cluster of five or six small florets or a large flower cane. Many weights have a shallow pocket of air above the canes which creates a silvery effect. The colours of Bacchus weights are generally muted by a very thin film of opaque white and this has given rise to the criticism, sometimes expressed, that Bacchus colours were pallid in comparison to the weights produced by other English glasshouses, but this seems to have been a deliberate conceit of the company and is a not unattractive feature of these weights. The quality of Bacchus weights is uneven. About a quarter of all Bacchus weights are poor in composition and finish, but the average weights were on par with those manufactured by Whitefriars in the comparable period, while the best of them were the equal of anything produced in France in the 1840s.

Bacchus also produced a few spaced or patterned millefiori weights on an opaque white ground which has been aptly described by J. P. Boore as sodden snow, from the tendency of the canes to sink into the somewhat muzzy surround. The patterns found in these weights are usually clusters of five or six canes about a small central cane, themselves grouped evenly across the ground, or small clusters grouped around a single large floret, itself surrounded by a ring of tiny florets. Very few carpet grounds were manufactured by Bacchus and those that have been recorded are poor in quality. Another very rare type of weight from Bacchus was the giant mushroom, almost four inches in diameter, with a

Concentric millefiori weight by Bacchus of Birmingham. 3½ in.

concentric tuft surrounded by torsades of flat spirals and latticinio. Two or three basket weights are known with clear glass overlays. A few encased overlays, similar to those produced by St Louis, are also recorded. Hollister also notes the existence of a single pedestal weight from Bacchus, a faceted concentric with green, pink and pale blue canes set in an opaque white basket.

It would be surprising if Bacchus had not manufactured other articles with a millefiori decoration, but apart from a pair of toilet bottles no related millefiori objects have so far been identified with this factory. Much research remains to be done on Bacchus and its products and such articles may eventually come to light.

ISLINGTON

That mine of information the *Art Journal* (February 1849) contains an intriguing note: "We have been much interested in examining some specimens of coloured, threaded and engraved glass, the productions of the Islington Glass Works, Birmingham, in which colours as brilliant and designs as elaborate as any seen in the Bohemian specimens were produced. The articles we have seen consisted of compound millefleur paperweights, coloured and engraved goblets, carafes and glass slabs of a most beautiful character in green and silver, adapted for finger plates and similar purposes. The whole of these specimens were little, if anything, inferior to the most choice productions of the Continent."

The Islington Glass Works referred to existed throughout much of the nineteenth century in Birmingham under various managements and various names. For much of this period it was under the direction of Rice Harris who was in partnership from 1822 to 1834 with William Gammon who subsequently became a partner in Bacchus. Rice Harris assumed major control of the Islington company about 1839 and over the ensuing twenty years he or his son exercised personal control of the firm. Rice Harris participated in the Birmingham Exhibition of 1849 and the Great Exhibition of 1851, though paperweights do not appear in the catalogues on either occasion among the articles produced by this glassworks. Apart from the intriguing reference in the *Art Journal* to "compound millefleur" the evidence for paperweight production rests entirely on two paperweights incorporating white canes with the initials IGW. From the range of different canes, including horse silhouettes and the fact that one is a close millefiori while the other is a spaced millefiori on a muslin ground, we can assume that Islington attained a high level of proficiency and versatility in this medium. The possibility that other Islington weights will turn up, as the existence of this company comes to the notice of more

A pinchbeck weight of a female saint playing a lyre among putti, surrounded by baroque scrollwork. 3 in.

Pinchbeck weight with
a silvery base moulded
in high relief. It shows
gallants and ladies on
and off horses in front
of a gate. $3\frac{1}{8}$ in.

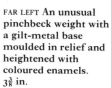

ABOVE Lovers on a
terrace; pinchbeck on
an alabaster base.
$3\frac{1}{4}$ in.

FAR LEFT An unusual
pinchbeck weight with
a gilt-metal base
moulded in relief and
heightened with
coloured enamels.
$3\frac{3}{8}$ in.

LEFT Pinchbeck weight
showing a cavalier
drinking beside his
horse with a girl at his
feet. $3\frac{1}{4}$ in.

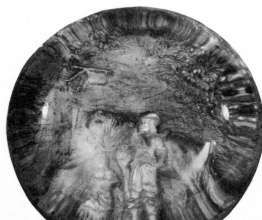

collectors, is highly likely. With the current revival of interest in paperweights it is to be hoped that more information and examples of its work become available.

KILNER

A type of paperweight peculiar to the British glasshouses was that made in green bottle glass, with a comparatively high dome and enclosing a representation of a flower or plant growing from a pot, the leaves and petals covered with masses of tiny silvery bubbles. The design was achieved by sprinkling chalk dust on the 'marver' (the base on which the paperweight was built up) and pressing over it a mass of soft green glass. A second layer of molten bottle glass was then pressed over it to enclose the chalk and the action of the heat produced the gaseous bubbles imparting to these weights their silvery, fairy-like appearance when held up to the light. Comparatively few of these 'bottle' weights bear an identifying mark, and they seem to have been produced all over England as a form of end-of-day work in the days when bottles were still largely made by hand. When bottles began to be machine-made the production of green paperweights died out. At one time they were so plentiful as not to excite the interest of collectors, but now they are rarely encountered and are regarded as worthy of the serious attention of collectors and students. It is thus worth hunting through drawers and the proverbial attic to which they may have long been relegated. Very large examples, weighing up to six pounds, were intended for use as door-stops rather than paperweights. Many of them do not have a floral motif, but merely a scatter of bubbles, whether by accident or design. A few have large upright sulphides of generally poor and coarse quality. These sulphide weights emanated largely from the Birmingham area and are mentioned in Chapter 2.

Though these large green weights were produced all over England they are always associated particularly with the West Riding of Yorkshire and it is here that they probably originated. Wakefield was an important centre of the bottle glass industry in the early nineteenth century and it is significant that the few inscribed weights which have been recorded bear the imprints of J. Tower or J. Kilner, both of whom operated glasshouses in that town.

John Kilner has given his name to the English language to denote a type of household storage jar. The traditional kilner jars, many of which are still doing yeoman service in kitchens all over the world, had a pronounced greenish tinge, like the old glass bottles which industrial archaeologists of the present day are forever excavating

An upright green bottle-glass weight by Kilner, showing a flowerpot containing 1 large and 3 small flowers.

on building sites and old rubbish tips. But Kilner's fortune was largely based on his output of bottles in the traditional dark green glass, and it was this material which served as the basis of the weights attributed to this factory. Although these weights were mainly produced by workmen from the glass left over at the end of the day it seems certain that Kilner regarded paperweights as an important by-product, proved by the comparatively large number of Kilner weights which bear an inscription. The inscription varies considerably, as the name of the company changed over the years, and this is a useful aid to dating these weights. The imprint appears on a thin glass wafer, applied to the base of the weight like a seal. John Kilner established a glasshouse at Whitwood Mere, Yorkshire in 1829 and it is to this period that those weights inscribed 'J. Kilner, Maker' belong. A few years later he moved to Dewsbury, near Wakefield and formed a partnership with his sons. Weights inscribed 'J. Kilner & Sons' therefore date from the late 1830s to 1844 when the company changed its name to Kilner Brothers. Subsequent weights bear this inscription. The production of green weights continued sporadically until the 1920s and therefore spans a period of about a century and inevitably the quality and appearance of the weights varies considerably over that span. A few Kilner weights have the characteristic flattened globular appearance of classic weights, but many of them are relatively tall, standing up to eight inches high, with pointed domes. Others have a relatively large, rounded dome, tapering away to a base with a much smaller diameter. Some have a footed base but the majority of them have a flat, slightly concave, base. There is no appreciable difference between those signed weights which were deliberately produced by the company, and the unsigned end-of-day ware made by craftsmen for their own amusement. The latter probably included the weights inscribed 'Merry Christmas' or 'A Happy New Year', which are thought to have been made by individual workmen as gifts to friends and relatives.

The bottle glass paperweights of Yorkshire are a comparatively neglected form of folk art. The sulphide weights, with their crude busts of the great nineteenth century political antagonists, Disraeli and Gladstone, or patriotic sentiments celebrating the jubilees of Queen Victoria or the coronation of King Edward VII, have a certain quaintness and naivety which collectors are now finding irresistible. The large weights, used as door-stops, are seldom found in fine condition, on account of the rough usage to which they were subjected, but even the smaller weights are getting hard to find in a perfect state, pointing to the cavalier treatment they received. Familiarity breeds contempt, and there are several 69

Two so-called Stourbridge weights with latticinio and millefiori canes. Mid 19th century

Two bubble weights by
Wedgwood.

references to these weights having been used as ornaments on footpaths and in rockeries! A few of them have circular holes drilled in their bases, pointing to their use as bedknobs or newel posts.

In the 1930s the Kilner company was taken over by the Glass Trust and subsequently its products were confined to strictly utilitarian wares. With the current revival of interest in paperweights it seems strange that the traditional bottle-green weight has not been revived in its classic form, although, as noted later in this chapter, something akin to it is now being produced by Wedgwood.

PAINTED AND PINCHBECK WEIGHTS

Exceedingly little is known as yet about paperweights with a moulded plaster ground painted over in the style of portrait miniatures. As a class they are not very plentiful and were it not for their artless quality (compared with millefiori weights) they would undoubtedly fetch far higher prices than they do. The young Queen Victoria and the ageing Duke of Wellington were popular subjects for these painted weights, and this seems to point to the late 1840s and early 1850s as the period of their manufacture. Indeterminate landscapes and hunting scenes were also favoured, and a sizeable proportion of these weights have classical motifs or biblical subjects. No attempt has been made to assign these weights to any particular glasshouse and it is unlikely that after this gap in time much concrete information regarding their antecedents will come to light.

The same may be said for the so-called pinchbeck weights. Christopher Pinchbeck (1670–1732), who discovered the alloy of copper and zinc which simulated gold, gave his name to the English language as a synonym for anything cheap, tawdry and *ersatz*, but here at least pinchbeck means precious, as Evangeline Bergstrom put it in her article on these intriguing weights published in the *American Collector* in 1945. This term is used to denote a wide range of weights with a metal relief over a base composed of pewter, copper, marble, alabaster or some other substance. The glass magnifying dome is set on top of the weight in the usual fashion, but pinchbeck weights seldom have the three-dimensional effect created by the sulphide weights. Conversely many sulphides have the illusion of being made of silver, but this effect is created by the refraction of light from the surface of the sulphide. Although they have been neglected by collectors and despised as inferior to the millefiori weights, pinchbeck weights stand up well to critical examination and from the intricacy of their composition it seems that they were the deliberate and serious product of manufacturers, perhaps on the fringe of the industry specialising in jewellery and fine objects of vertu. Apart from Queen Victoria, whose portrait bobbed up everywhere in the mid-nineteenth century, the subjects of these pinchbeck weights are generally unidentifiable, and the majority of weights preferred timeless and classless scenes of family life and domestic occupations, as well as the biblical and mythological vignettes found on painted weights. Mrs Bergstrom records a pinchbeck weight, of a lion attacking two horses at a waterhole, bearing the inscription 'G. & S. Lobmeyr, Wien', thus indicating that some at least of these pinchbeck weights were manufactured on the Continent as well as in Britain. Indeed, the fact that no English glasshouse has been labelled, even by tradition, as the manufacturer of pinchbeck weights, should undermine the confident attribution of these weights to England. J. & L. Lobmeyr was formerly one of the most important glassmakers of Bohemia

Wedgwood weight in the shape of a 'Tawny Owl'.

and the above-mentioned firm was probably a Viennese offshoot. Since 1918, when Bohemia severed its connection with Austria, J. & L. Lobmeyr have developed into the leading Austrian glass-works, but although its products have included some of the finest engraved and enamelled glass produced this century, paperweights have not featured in its extensive repertoire. For the time being, at any rate, collectors will continue to regard pinchbeck paperweights as an English phenomenon.

OTHER NINETEENTH CENTURY PAPERWEIGHTS

While most countries concentrated on the millefiori paperweight, and occasional forays into fruit and flower weights and sulphides, the English manufacturers seem to have shown the greatest diversification, if not inventiveness, in the range of paperweights they produced. Unfortunately the bulk of them were intended for a mass market and were inexpensive gimcrack baubles which only now are beginning to excite the interest of collectors, largely on the grounds of age and quaintness. Of the more interesting and better produced weights in this class perhaps the so-called hollow weights may eventually be regarded as highly as the bottle-green weights, if no higher. They consist of a hollow sphere enclosing a relatively flat ground with an impressed cameo or intaglio design of clear or coloured glass. The intervening space between the ground and the casing often creates a silvery effect which is quite pleasing. Because these weights are only now attracting the attention of collectors nothing is known of their origins, though Stevens & Williams, Richardson or Webb, all glass manufacturers of the Stourbridge area, have been tentatively named as likely producers of such weights.

Charles Colné's report of 1878 mentions the London firm of James Green as producing paperweights in cut or engraved glass, but this reference is too vague to serve as the basis for positive attribution of weights to this firm. Apart from the sulphides, mentioned in Chapter 2, clear glass cameos set in globes with flattened bases have been recorded in connection with the celebration of Queen Victoria's Diamond Jubilee in 1897, but nothing

Wedgwood weight known as 'The Trout'.

is known of their antecedents. Then there are the clear glass oblongs with rounded corners which were a popular souvenir of holiday resorts and tourist attractions around the turn of the century. To the *afficionado* of paperweights in the classic tradition these objects are an abomination, yet they have been promoted in recent years to the status of collectability as yet another example of late Victorian knick-knackery. For that reason alone they have been collected and now fetch prices beyond that of many modern paperweights whose aesthetic appeal is infinitely greater. They contain a transfer print, sometimes from an engraving but more usually from a tinted sepia photograph, mounted on the base and covered by a rectangle of clear glass which serves to magnify the picture though not to the extent found in the domed classic weights. These weights, machine made at every stage of their production, lack the endearing qualities possessed by the bottle-green weights or the artistry of the millefiori weights. As mementoes of that vanished era which preceded the First World War they have a certain nostalgic ring and are just as worthy of collecting and preservation as analogous subjects like picture postcards and match-box labels.

Alum Bay, at the western end of the Isle of Wight, has long been famous for its curious cliff formation and the many different colours of sand found on the beach below. From the middle of the nineteenth century onwards tourists have visited Alum Bay to collect specimens of pebbles and sand in a wide variety of hues. This encouraged an industry, which flourishes to this day, producing souvenirs which incorporate the variegated sand. Most of these souvenirs take the form of sand pictures and glass objects containing layers of different coloured sand, and inevitably the latter have included paperweights. Many of these are straightforward hemispheres in the paperweight tradition but a few of the more elaborate weights are tower-shaped and sometimes incorporate a transfer print of some local beauty spot or tourist landmark, such as the Needles or Carisbrooke Castle. These Alum Bay paperweights were mainly produced in the period from 1880 to 1914 but there has been a revival of interest in them in recent years and it is to this modern period that the plainer weights belong.

WEDGWOOD

King's Lynn in Norfolk was a glassmaking centre as long ago as the seventeenth century and specialised in a distinctive type of drinking glass with narrow horizontal corrugations. During the nineteenth century, however, the industry went into decline and had died out by the 1890s. In 1967 Josiah Wedgwood and Sons, the

A many-faceted pyramid weight by Wedgwood, there are several choices of colour for the double ball inside.

73

Staffordshire pottery firm, decided to diversify into glassware and chose King's Lynn as the site of this enterprise. Ronald Stennett-Willson, head of the industrial glass department at the Royal College of Art, was appointed managing director of King's Lynn Glass Ltd, and glassblowers were recruited from Sweden, Austria and Germany as well as from Great Britain. Not surprisingly the products of this factory show a strong affinity with modern Scandinavian designs. Apart from table wares such as glasses, goblets, decanters and bowls, King's Lynn Glass have entered the paperweight field.

In the modern Swedish and Norwegian style Wedgwood first produced, in August 1970, a penguin in jewelled tones of blue, amethyst or topaz, with a broad paperweight base. Since then several other bird weights have been manufactured, either in clear glass or in opaque glass with a coloured spatter simulating plumage. In 1972 a paperweight fish was added to the range. It gleams in freshwater colouring of blue-green and browns shading into translucency, the colour being captured inside clear glass.

Echoing the designs of Orrefors and Kosta, Wedgwood also released a Valentine paperweight in 1970. The heart-shaped weight, designed by Stennett-Willson, stands three inches tall and contains an inverted heart-shaped tear. Subsequently large bullet-shaped weights have been produced with intriguing patterns of tears and bubbles. In 1971 a faceted paperweight in clear glass, incorporating one or more globules of coloured glass, was introduced.

OTHER MODERN ENGLISH WEIGHTS
Though no traditions of paperweight production in Stourbridge in the nineteenth century have been substantiated, at least one firm in this area has embarked on the manufacture of weights in recent years. Webb Corbett have recently experimented with large 'door-stop' paperweights in colourless clear glass with an overall spaced bubble pattern enclosing a spiral coloured glass cage in which is trapped a large bubble. The effect is unusual and most pleasing. Several firms and individual craftsmen have begun experimenting with real flowers trapped in glass. Rosabelle are producing traditional weights, enclosing actual roses using a secret technique. Some of these weights have a flat, slightly concave base, while others have a footed base. Other weights now on the market make use of everlasting daisies and other dried flowers encapsulated in a similar fashion. It remains to be seen, however, to what extent this combination of nature with craftsmanship will appeal to the collecting public.

English blue millefiori ink bottle, mid 19th century.

BELOW A pinchbeck weight of an unknown lady. (SPINK & SON)

ABOVE A Kilner 'flower-pot' weight, the motif being rendered by bubbles trapped in the glass. There are 6 flowers with red centres.

RIGHT English pink millefiori ink bottle, mid 19th century

ABOVE A so-called
Stourbridge millefiori
weight, dated 1847.

ABOVE RIGHT Coronation
weight with E II R 1953
on central cane, by
Powells of Wealdstone
(now Whitefriars).

RIGHT A faceted
millefiori weight by
Whitefriars. Note the
'White Friar' symbol
on one cane.

BELOW A Whitefriars
door-stop weight.

A scattered millefiori
weight of the mid 19th
century.

A mass-produced
tourist weight, showing
Portree, Isle of Skye.

ABOVE A flower on a latticinio basket ground. Note the initial P cane, 1973.

LEFT A scattered millefiori and latticinio weight by Paul Ysart.

Upright flower weight by Strathearn. Note the S cane.

FAR LEFT An abstract weight by Caithness called 'Moon-landing' and commemorating the landing of Apollo XI.

ABOVE A ribbon weight with a rose centre by Perthshire.

BELOW A close millefiori weight by Perthshire, dated 1973 and signed P.

BELOW RIGHT Silhouette canes of animals including a squirrel and a puffin on a latticinio ground by Perthshire.

BELOW A dragonfly weight with millefiori border, made in 1970 by Perthshire.

BELOW A large
strawberry weight by
Mount Washington,
only five of these were
ever made. $4\frac{1}{8}$ in.
(COURTESY BERGSTROM
ART CENTER)

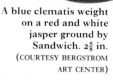

A diamond-cut red and
white marbrie weight
with red flower
attributed to the New
England Glass Co.
$3\frac{3}{8}$ in. (COURTESY
BERGSTROM ART CENTER)

A blue clematis weight
on a red and white
jasper ground by
Sandwich. $2\frac{5}{8}$ in.
(COURTESY BERGSTROM
ART CENTER)

A cluster of fruit
weight by Sandwich
with a concave base.
$3\frac{1}{8}$ in. (COURTESY
BERGSTROM ART CENTER)

BELOW A small flat
spray weight with a
millefiori basket by the
New England Glass Co.
$3\frac{1}{16}$ in. (COURTESY
BERGSTROM ART CENTER)

BELOW A white and
lavender rose weight
with berries and
butterfly by Mount
Washington. $4\frac{1}{4}$ in.
(COURTESY BERGSTROM
ART CENTER)

A flower weight by
Sandwich which has
been attributed to
Nicolas Lutz. $2\frac{7}{8}$ in.
(COURTESY BERGSTROM
ART CENTER)

Ten

Scottish Paperweights

Glassmaking has been an important industry in Scotland since the seventeenth century, but the bulk of production was confined to industrial glass and domestic tableware. There was little tradition of ornamental glassmaking in Scotland prior to the present century and most of that has resulted from the influx of ideas and techniques from other countries. Nevertheless a certain amount of decorative glass was produced, though at this distance in time it is difficult to pinpoint it to any particular glasshouse. No Scottish company is known to have made paperweights, either in the millefiori style of Bacchus or the bottle-green dumps favoured by the Yorkshire glassworkers, though John Ford of Edinburgh made sulphide weights portraying Robert Burns and other Scottish celebrities.

There is, however, in the Victoria and Albert Museum an intriguing paperweight of unusual design. It is made of clear colourless crystal and consists of an obelisk rising from a heavy rectangular base. The glass, cut on a wheel, is of excellent workmanship and is thought to date from the middle of the nineteenth century and to be of Edinburgh origin. The base is inscribed with a diamond point 'Queen Mary's Sun Dial Holyrood Palace'. The City of Glasgow Art Galleries and Museum has an extensive collection of Scottish glass marbles, some of which are several inches in diameter and exhibit the swirls and striations of opaque and coloured glass often associated with German marbles of the second half of the nineteenth century. The same techniques could easily have been applied to paperweights, but there is, as yet, no evidence of this.

Although traditions of paperweight making in Scotland are almost totally absent, it is in Scotland that the finest British paperweights have been produced this century. Credit for this rests mainly on one man, Paul Ysart, whose contribution to the art of modern paperweights is unequalled anywhere in the world. Ysart was born in Barcelona in 1904 of Bohemian parentage. He moved with his family to France before the First World War and his father Salvadore learned the techniques of glassblowing, possibly at St Louis. This is no more than surmise, though a miniature St Louis weight has been recorded in the style favoured by the early Ysart weights. In 1915 his father moved to Scotland where he obtained employment at the Leith Flint Glassworks which specialised in scientific and industrial glassware. His son Paul subsequently joined him and for a time worked on scientific glass.

Perthshire's Christmas 1971 weight with holly motif. (Edition of 250)

Amethyst overlay scent bottle by Perthshire, dated 1972 on the base. (Edition of 300)

79

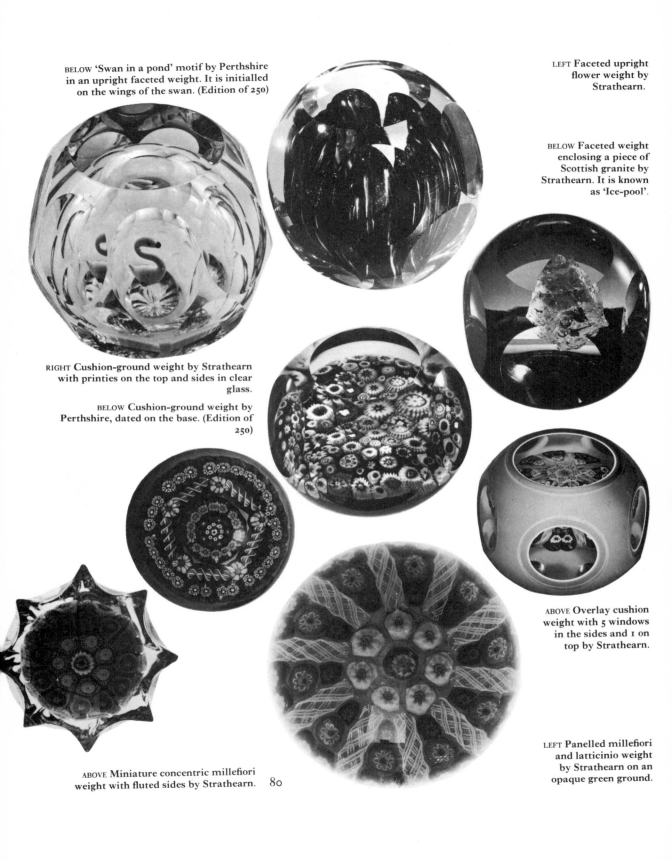

BELOW 'Swan in a pond' motif by Perthshire in an upright faceted weight. It is initialled on the wings of the swan. (Edition of 250)

LEFT Faceted upright flower weight by Strathearn.

BELOW Faceted weight enclosing a piece of Scottish granite by Strathearn. It is known as 'Ice-pool'.

RIGHT Cushion-ground weight by Strathearn with printies on the top and sides in clear glass.

BELOW Cushion-ground weight by Perthshire, dated on the base. (Edition of 250)

ABOVE Overlay cushion weight with 5 windows in the sides and 1 on top by Strathearn.

ABOVE Miniature concentric millefiori weight with fluted sides by Strathearn.

LEFT Panelled millefiori and latticinio weight by Strathearn on an opaque green ground.

In the 1920s Ysart began making paperweights in traditional millefiori patterns. These consisted of concentric, spaced, garland or patterned millefiori designs on a wide variety of grounds, some translucent in shades of deep blue, green, red or purple, and others mottled and opaque in shades ranging from pale pink to sandy yellow and flaming orange. A peculiarly Ysart technique was his use of lengths of filigree cane sunk into the ground. The millefiori canes themselves are well up to the standard of the classic French weights. The majority of weights by Paul Ysart incorporate a cane initialled PY.

Ysart has also made a number of flower and insect weights, always in a flat, two-dimensional style, unlike the upright weights of his American contemporary Charles Kaziun. Of these the best are undoubtedly his butterflies and dragonflies in coloured glass with a millefiori surround. Sometimes millefiori canes are used to make the bodies and wings of these insects. For much of his working life Paul Ysart lived in Perthshire but in the past decade has moved to Caithness in the far north of Scotland. It is no coincidence that Perthshire and Caithness are, today, the two centres of paperweight manufacture in Scotland. More recent Ysart weights not only contain the PY cane, but often have the word 'Caithness' inscribed in their base.

Other members of the Ysart family worked with Jim Moncrieff for many years at a glassworks in Perth and evolved the distinctive type of glassware known as Monart. Eventually the family decided to start its own small factory in Perth. This traded as Ysart Brothers and latterly as Vasart Glass Ltd. This company continued to make vases and bowls in the Monart tradition, but also produced glass paperweights and related millefiori articles such as door knobs, corkscrews and other cocktail equipment. In 1963 the Scotch whisky distilling firm of William Teacher & Sons conceived a publicity gimmick in the form of one of their whisky bottles, complete with label and cap, but squashed flat into the form of a dish. They had considerable difficulty in finding a manufacturer for this idea but eventually they offered the problem to Vasart who achieved success and won the contract.

During their discussions with Vasart and various visits to Perth to watch the progress of the project, executives of Teacher's became fascinated with the craft of glassblowing. At the same time they realised that if this enterprising glassworks was to survive in the competitive atmosphere of the modern glass industry it would require financial support. It seemed natural that a company engaged in one traditional Scottish industry should support another, and out of this mutual co-operation grew the Strathearn Glass Com-

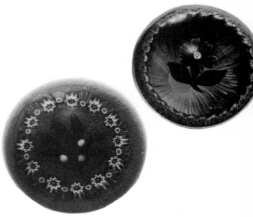

TOP A pink-leaved dahlia weight by Perthshire, faceted on 4 sides and dated 1972 on the base. (Edition of 200)

CENTRE Small flower in a basket by Perthshire, with initial P cane in centre.

ABOVE Perthshire's Christmas 1972 weight showing mistletoe on a red ground. (Edition of 300)

BELOW Faceted cushion-ground weight by Perthshire, dated 1972 on the base. (Edition of 300)

Upright faceted weight by Strathearn with seaweed motif.

pany, in which Teacher's became the majority shareholders. The firm's operations were transferred to the neighbouring town of Crieff and production began in December 1964.

Strathearn Glass continued initially to make the range of glassware hitherto produced by Vasart but have added other pieces in the idiom of the great glasshouses of the nineteenth century. They make the full range of the traditional weights in a variety of sizes from miniature to jumbo (magnum) in unlimited editions. These include scrambled, concentric, carpet and patterned millefiori, spaced millefiori on a lace (muslin) ground, overlays, butterfly and flower weights. At the same time small, limited, quality editions of crown and overlay weights are also produced for collectors. These limited editions incorporate an S initial cane and have the year of manufacture inscribed upon them. They also produce a range with distinctive styles and names to match. 'Stoer' is the name given to a weight enclosing Scottish sand and ground gravel. 'Ice Pool' has a chunk of Scottish quartz floating in a clear glass hemisphere. Many, though not all, Strathearn weights incorporate a cane with the initial S.

Another glasshouse, known as Perthshire Paperweights, was established at Crieff in 1968 by a group of craftsmen from Vasart under the direction of Stuart Drysdale, a former director of Vasart, because they disliked the policy of the new management. Drysdale and his craftsmen wished to continue making traditional weights of the very highest quality and have certainly achieved this aim. Perthshire Paperweights rapidly acquired a reputation for maintaining the highest standards of technique and finish; their limited editions are widely accepted to be among the finest of modern weights. Jack Allan and Anton Moravec have specialised in dated overlay weights and subject weights featuring dragonflies and other

LEFT Faceted pansy weight by Perthshire with millefiori surround, 1971.

RIGHT Side view of Paul Ysart's barber-pole weight.

insects. These weights are engraved on the base with the date and the initials JA and AM and are sold with a numbered certificate. They have produced several Christmas weights in limited editions and usually produce three or four limited editions per year. They also make a range of millefiori and flat insect weights in an unlimited edition. Some Perthshire weights incorporate a P initial cane. A feature of some of the paperweights by this company is the dead flat base with a star-cut ornament in the centre.

Glassmaking has become one of the most important industries in Caithness in recent years, the emphasis being on high quality lead glass in a wide range of decorative and useful wares. In 1971 Caithness Glass, of Harrowhill, Wick, began producing paperweights. Though the profiles are the traditional flattened globes the motifs are quite unlike anything that has gone before. One weight, in an unlimited edition, for example, has a surrealist quality suggesting the flame, gases and molten lava bubbling on the surface of a volcano. Others, in limited editions, are designed by Colin Terris and hand-made by Peter Holmes. The two weights being marketed in 1972 had a space motif. 'Starbase' has an abstract design symbolising a space station of the future spinning in outer space, with the planet Earth below. 'Orbit' is an abstract interpretation of the unknown we may one day discover in the exploration of outer space. The silvery ring represents a space vehicle in orbit above the surface of an unknown planet. Viewing these fascinating weights from different angles, and letting the light fall on the strange moonscape and spatial atmosphere, we are looking at something magic – scarcely anything so mundane as glass. In the Caithness paperweights of the nineteen seventies we can see the shape of things to come – a far cry from the close millefiori of Baccarat or Bohemia.

Scattered 'barber-pole' canes on an opaque white ground by Paul Ysart.

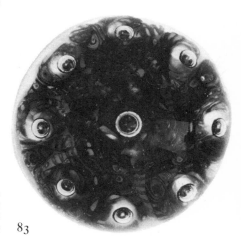

LEFT Side view of a faceted overlay weight by Perthshire, dated 1970. (Edition of 150)

83

American Paperweights

BELOW A rose weight on a white latticinio ground by Sandwich. $2\frac{7}{8}$ in.

BOTTOM A pink flower weight on a white latticinio ground by Sandwich. $3\frac{1}{16}$ in.

Unlike Europe America remained constant to the glass paperweight. These attractive novelties came to the United States in the 1850s, when they were already on the wane in France and continued to be produced for a discerning public right down to the present day, though their popularity fluctuated considerably in that period of 120 years. During that time three companies have been responsible for the majority of American weights, while half a dozen others have made them at one time or another, and the tradition of fine paperweights is carried on at the present day by a number of master craftsmen, while several of the major glass companies are now experimenting with weights which depart from the traditional form and content. The study of glass in general and paperweights in particular has always been strongest in the United States and it would be interesting to speculate how far the American market has stimulated paperweight production in Britain and Europe. Regretably the trade has not been two-way and relatively few American weights ever find their way across the Atlantic. Consequently they are seldom seen in European antique shops or in the salerooms and their interest to collectors outside their native land is largely academic.

It is popularly believed that the glass paperweight came to America in 1851 when visitors to the Great Exhibition in London would have had the opportunity to see these baubles on display. Significantly the earliest dated American weight is of that year and features the profiles of Queen Victoria and her Consort. But this theory is too presumptuous and it is just as likely that Americans travelling on the Continent of Europe in the late 1840s saw and purchased examples of the paperweights of Murano, Bohemia and France. European styles influenced early American paperweights and European migrants in the glasshouses of New England exerted a powerful influence in the techniques adopted there. Consequently early American weights tend to follow European examples, but native ingenuity and independent spirit inevitably combined to produce some distinctive styles.

THE NEW ENGLAND GLASS COMPANY

Glassmaking was established in Cambridge, Massachusetts in the seventeenth century but the company which outshone its competitors, and is sometimes referred to as *the* Cambridge glassworks, was founded only in 1818 as the New England Glass Company by a group of men who included Deming Jarves, later to branch out on his own with the rival Sandwich company. The NEGC, as it is often abbreviated, rapidly became one of the leading producers of flint glass in the United States, in a versatile range of articles ranging from electric insulators to ecclesiastical chandeliers. At an early stage the company began producing decorative glassware, being in the forefront of the art glass movement and turning out excellent engraved glass and pressed glass. The company was a valuable training ground for other companies. Several of its personnel subsequently set up as glass manufacturers on their own account. The firm was taken over in 1878 by William Libbey whose son, Edward Drummond Libbey, transferred the plant and many of its employees to Toledo, Ohio in 1888 following a disastrous industrial dispute. Glass paperweights were produced by the New England Glass Company over a period of thirty years (1850–80).

One of the first – if not the first – weights produced by this company was a hexagonal pressed glass weight containing a reproduction of William Wyon's medal of 1851 showing the conjoined profiles of Queen Victoria and Prince Albert. The antecedents of this curious weight are unknown, though it was for many years in the possession of the Hopkins family who were glassworkers at Cambridge. Hollister tentatively assigns this important documentary piece to Thomas Hopkins whose niece had this paperweight some eighty years after it was made. The bulk of the NEGC weights seem to have been made in the period from 1854 to 1874. Among the craftsmen who are known to have made paperweights during this period perhaps the best was Frank Pierre (1834–72), an Alsatian who served his apprenticeship at Baccarat and worked at the New England Glass Company from 1849 till his premature death. To him is given the credit for producing the best millefiori weights as well as many of the blown fruit weights which were a Cambridge speciality. Thomas Leighton (1786–1849) hailed from Birmingham, as did William Gillinder; and George and Robert Dale emigrated from Leith, Scotland to New England in 1830. Thus, during its heyday, Cambridge drew heavily on French and British techniques and inspiration, hence the confusion which often arises in identifying its weights. Moreover Gillinder and others moved around the United States, from company to company, and often used the same canes and methods of production, so that the attribution of many American weights is problematical. It is difficult to speak dogmatically about paperweight profiles and characteristic canes when speaking of the American companies.

Paperweights of the New England Glass Company did not have a single distinctive profile. All that can be said, by way of identifica-

Floral plaque weight with a red ribbon bow by Mount Washington. $5\frac{1}{4} \times 3\frac{1}{2}$ in. (CHRISTIES)

A rectangular flat bouquet weight with a pink and white ribbon tying the stems by Mount Washington. $5\frac{3}{16} \times 3\frac{1}{2}$ in.

85

TOP A hollow crown weight with red-and-green and pink-and-white ribbons with central cane bearing date 1825; made by Sandwich about 1856. 2⅜ in.

ABOVE A double-overlay weight enclosing a pattern of millefiori over a white latticinio cushion by the New England Glass Co, the overlays are red and white. 2⅞ in.

BELOW A purple flower weight on a white latticinio ground with faceted and fluted top and two rows of printies in the sides by the New England Glass Co. 2½ in.

86

tion, is that they have a very deep basal concavity – far deeper than the paperweights of any other company. Profiles may be either high or low, facetting may consist of vertical fluting, alternating with small printies, or multiple printies alone, and sometimes a group of four interlocking printies across the top. Occasionally small 'crows feet' cuts may be found between large printies. The clear glass sometimes has a slight smoky or pink tinge.

Very few dated weights were produced by this company. Lura Watkins, in her book *Cambridge Glass*, records several dated 1852 and a single millefiori weight dated 1854. No weights were identified by initialled canes. The greatest source of confusion is the fact that Cambridge used virtually the same canes as Sandwich, its greatest rival. The only way of telling them apart is to examine the base, where the deep concavity and the irregularity of the endings of the canes are Cambridge hallmarks. It is likely that the leading American companies imported many of their millefiori canes from Europe and Bohemia and Baccarat have been put forward as the likeliest sources. Certainly many of the canes found in the weights of Cambridge and Sandwich bear a resemblance to those found in Baccarat and Bohemian paperweights, especially the silhouette canes, though usually these are somewhat distorted in the American versions as a result of technical differences in the fusion of the glass.

Cambridge produced scrambled millefiori weights which resemble a macedoine of fruits, all jumbled up together with fragments of latticinio. A few indeterminate blue, brown or green coloured grounds have been noted in connection with these weights but the majority are on clear grounds. Cambridge manufactured a few concentrics with the circles close together, and a larger number in which the circles were spaced out. In both cases the circles were invariably of identical canes. The open concentrics often had a base of double-swirled latticinio. A handful of concentrics have a spoked wheel pattern created by canes spaced outside the circles. Cambridge produced a few crown weights which are sometimes mistaken for St Louis crowns. They are not so tightly packed as their French counterparts and have a heavier outer casing. Cambridge made a few paperweights with coloured or carpet grounds. The coloured grounds were not very successful, but the carpet weights are most attractive in their simplicity. Usually they have a carpet of canes of the same colour, with a single silhouette in the centre. Among the rarest weights from this factory are the double overlays containing a mushroom of millefiori. These beautiful weights attained the acme of perfection in their canes, set-up, lampwork, cutting and overlays.

Emulating St Louis, Cambridge made a few flat bouquet weights with a cluster of millefiori blossoms and green leaves on a double-

swirled latticinio base. Among the identifiable flowers found in Cambridge weights may be mentioned the yellow clematis, the bright red poinsettia and the occasional buttercup. All of these flower weights are extremely rare. There are also a few fruit basket weights, generally poor in composition and finish, and probably regarded by Cambridge as experimental.

The greatest contribution of this company to the art of the paper-weight was undoubtedly its blown fruit weights. The majority of them were apples and pears, either free standing or mounted on a clear 'cookie' base. The majority had a clear glass surround but a few seem to have been dipped in opaque glass of various colours and have thus acquired a curious mottled effect. It is probable that Cambridge derived their fruit weights from Venice where such novelties were in existence early in the eighteenth century and were being produced in the mid-nineteenth century. Somewhat similar weights are being made in Czechoslovakia to this day.

SANDWICH PAPERWEIGHTS

In 1825 Deming Jarves left Cambridge to found the Boston and Sandwich Glass Company of Sandwich, Massachusetts and generally known to collectors as Sandwich. By the middle of the 1850s the Sandwich company was as large as the Cambridge glassworks and from then onwards the history of the two companies is strangely parallel. Jarves left Sandwich in 1858 and founded the

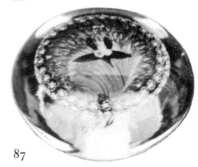

87

A flat pressed weight by Gillinder & Sons with a frosted intaglio profile bust of Abraham Lincoln. $3\frac{1}{4}$ in.

A triple pig weight with pebble-ground by Philip Bunamo at Union Glass about 1910. $3\frac{7}{8}$ in.

BELOW A signed 'under sea' doorstop by Tiffany. $4\frac{15}{16}$ in.

A sulphide portrait weight of about 1865 showing Robert E. Lee, above a swirl cushion of red, white and blue. $2\frac{5}{16}$ in.

A lily weight with white petals mottled in red and pink, attributed to the Ravenna Glass Co. $3\frac{1}{2}$ in.

88

Cape Cod Glass Company which closed down in 1869. Like Cambridge, Sandwich was faced by labour disputes and rising costs which eventually forced it out of business in 1888. The majority of the paperweights made at Sandwich are thought to date from the 1870s, though a few dated weights are known which were produced in the 1850s. Edmund Rice and an Austrian immigrant known as Timothy Collins are alleged to have produced the finest weights in the early period, while Nicholas Lutz (1835–1904) is credited with the fine weights of the later period. Lutz served his apprenticeship at St Louis where he was born and came to the United States in 1860. Originally he worked for Christian Dorflinger at the Green Point Glass Works in Brooklyn, New York, but subsequently found employment at White Mills, Pennsylvania and the New England Glass Company. He moved from Cambridge to Sandwich in 1869 and worked there until the firm closed down in 1888. In his last years he worked at the Mount Washington Glassworks and finally the Union Glass Company at Somerville. Such is the high esteem in which Lutz's work is held that collectors pay enhanced prices for weights attributed to him. Yet only one weight has so far been discovered which is incontrovertibly his work and bears his signature. In this weight the lettering trails like tendrils through the foliage of a flower.

Like Cambridge, Sandwich produced paperweights in a wide variety of shapes and profiles with a low, flat crown predominating. Generally speaking Sandwich weights are lighter than those of other American firms and the quality of the glass varied considerably in clarity. As has already been stated there is little appreciable difference in the canes used by Sandwich and Cambridge with, perhaps, a greater range of colours in the paperweights of the former and a predilection for opaque white canes which throw the coloured canes into sharp contrast. The majority of Sandwich weights were of the scrambled millefiori type with the same pell-mell mixture found in Cambridge weights. A few of these weights include canes bearing the date 1852 or 1825. Mrs Bergstrom, in *Old Glass Paperweights*, put forward the theory that the weights with the latter date were, in fact, 1852 weights with the digits transposed by accident, but Hollister points out that 1825 was the year in which the company was formed and therefore these weights may have been intended to celebrate the anniversary of the foundation. A very few patterned millefiori weights were made at Sandwich and are regarded as belonging to the early period.

Sandwich was renowned for its beautiful flower weights, which are thought to have been the speciality of Nicholas Lutz. Poinsettias were, by far, the commonest flowers, but others included the

A white lily weight surrounded by five trumpet flowers, attributed to the Ravenna Glass Co. 3½ in.

so-called Sandwich weedflower, a wheatflower and flowers with striped petals. A solitary rose-bush weight has been recorded and attributed to this company. Among the rarities of Sandwich are the remarkable upright floral bouquets credited to Lutz, though some authorities are sceptical and are now inclined to assign these weights to the New England Glass Company. Sandwich also made a few paperweights showing baskets of mixed fruit. Of doubtful origin are the blown fruit weights occasionally attributed to Sandwich. They may in fact have been made by Lutz during the two-year period (1867–9) when he was employed at Cambridge. The same may be said of the white deer and swans in hollow blown glass. A few flower weights, have a marbrie background but it is now conjectured that Lutz made these weights while working at Somerville. Much of the information relating to Lutz and his work is derived from the extensive collection of the Lutz family and at this point of time it is often difficult to say at what stage in his career he made certain paperweights.

GILLINDER

One of the most remarkable men in the American glass industry of the nineteenth century was William T. Gillinder, who was something of an infant prodigy. He began his apprenticeship at the age of eight and was a gaffer (foreman) at the age of twenty. At 28 he became secretary of the National Flint Glass Makers Society of Great Britain and Ireland and two years later he left his native country to take up an appointment at the New England Glass Company. In England Gillinder made paperweights, possibly for Bacchus of Birmingham, and subsequently he studied the art under Frank Pierre before moving on to other factories. After numerous changes of employment in the late 1850s he settled down in Philadelphia in 1861 and founded his own factory. In 1867 the company became Gillinder & Sons and four years later he died, leaving his sons James and Frederick to carry on the business. Gillinder's took a prominent part in the Philadelphia Centennial Exposition of 1876. In 1888 or 1889 the company moved to Greensburg, Pennsylvania and subsequently was absorbed by the United States Glass Company. Thenceforward the company seems to have specialised in lamps of every kind. In 1912 James Gillinder's three sons formed a new company, called Gillinder Brothers at Port Jervis, New York and this firm is still in operation.

William Gillinder's American paperweights date from the decade 1861 to 1871 and for the most part had a distinctive high-domed profile cut with deep oval printies. After his death his sons produced paperweights in various shapes – not only circular and oval but

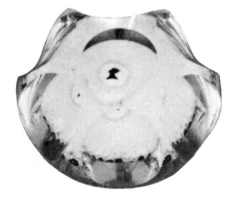

A faceted concentric millefiori weight with central silhouette cane, made by Gillinder & Sons. $3\frac{3}{16}$ in.

hexagonal and in the shape of animals. A collection of Gillinder canes has been preserved in the Toledo Museum of Art and consists mostly of crimped canes, cogs and ruffles. A female profile is known as a silhouette cane and this has been variously identified as Queen Victoria or Jenny Lind, the 'Swedish nightingale'. Most of the early Gillinder weights consist of concentric millefiori or carpet grounds, both of outstanding quality and superb in design and finish. Gillinder made one or two flower weights reminiscent of Cambridge.

The later Gillinder weights, prominent at the time of the Centennial Exposition, consist mainly of clear glass weights with profiles of George Washington, Benjamin Franklin and Abraham Lincoln intaglio-impressed into the base. Some of these weights are inscribed 'Gillinder & Sons, Centennial Exhibition, Phila., 1876' and bear a striking resemblance in format and style to the Cambridge Victoria and Albert weight of 1851. Gillinder's also produced a number of rectangular glass weights commemorating the Exposition, and featuring pictures of the Exposition buildings and landmarks in paper stuck to the base. These are not in the same class as the other Gillinder weights but are interesting as early examples of the 'seaside resort' weights which became so popular towards the end of the nineteenth century.

Gillinder also produced moulded glass weights in the form of animals, birds and flowers, no doubt inspired by the similar weights made by the New England Glass Company about the same period and the moulded animal figures of Clarence Heisey which were popular in the late nineteenth century. The Gillinder animal weights may be found in clear glass or in opaque black or white glass.

Some confusion has been caused in the past through the similarity of the name Gilliland with Gillinder. John L. Gilliland and Company of Brooklyn, New York, were manufacturers of fine glassware in the period from 1820 to 1860 and formerly many American paperweights were attributed to this factory. A more critical appraisal of American paperweights in recent years, however, has scotched the Gilliland theory. This firm *may* have made paperweights, but so far no weights have been produced to substantiate the assertion that they did.

MOUNT WASHINGTON

The Mount Washington Glass Works, one of the most famous in the annals of American nineteenth century art glass, also produced paperweights which, though relatively few in number, are outstanding in form and composition. The glassworks was founded by Deming Jarves in 1837, supposedly on behalf of his son George

BELOW A 'devil's fire' weight in blue and red on a mottled ground, made at Millville and attributed to Marcus Kuntz. 3$\frac{9}{16}$ in.
CENTRE A pink lily weight signed 'Steuben 1941' on the base and made at Corning in that year. 3$\frac{3}{16}$ in.

A weight with a cross on a mound and foliage with the words 'Rock of Ages' above in opaque white, six red spots on the cross, attributed to Millville. 3$\frac{1}{4}$ in.

(1825–50). Young Jarves died very young and it is presumed that he had little influence on the conduct of the business. By 1856 the firm was taken over by two of its former employees, William Libbey and Timothy Howe. Libbey became sole proprietor in 1866 and moved the company to New Bedford in 1869. Subsequently the firm became known as W. L. Libbey & Co and was involved in the later history of the New England Glass Company. The original name was resumed in 1871 but in 1894 the Mount Washington Company was taken over by the Pair point Manufacturing Company. In the present century the company had several changes of location, management and name and ended up as the Pairpoint Glass Works in 1957. The company went out of business the following year.

The best paperweights associated with Mount Washington were produced in the period between 1869 and 1876 and are known to collectors as the Mount Washington Roses. These huge weights, measuring up to $4\frac{1}{2}$ inches in diameter, contain the finest attempt at roses ever made in glass, though the effect is somewhat reduced by the inclusion of some unnatural looking butterflies and occasionally a pygmy hand grasping the stem. These rose weights were low crowned, two-dimensional affairs. One or two have been recorded with facets ground in the top and sides. Apart from the roses, Mount Washington produced paperweights containing poinsettias, dahlias

LEFT A spherical pink rose weight mounted on a stand and made by Ralph Barber at Whitall Tatum & Co. Millville. $3\frac{1}{2}$ in, 6 in high.

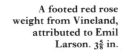

A footed red rose weight from Vineland, attributed to Emil Larson. $3\frac{5}{8}$ in.

BELOW A footed pink and white striped rose weight in dark green glass. $2\frac{15}{16}$ in.

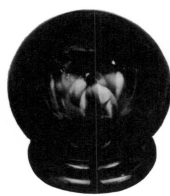

and flowering fruits (plums or grapes). Several weights incorporating groups of strawberries have been recorded. A few large rectangular weights containing bouquets of flowers are known. These flower plaques have the decorative motif set in a chamfered rectangle of clear glass about an inch thick and measuring $3\frac{1}{2}$ inches by 5 inches. A unique plaque containing a cluster of four wild strawberries completes the range of these extraordinary plaque weights.

An account of this company would not be complete without a reference to the large footed spiral weights manufactured in the decade before the First World War. They consist of a large solid globe mounted on a base. Within the globe is a spiral arrangement in opaque white with deep blue or red contrasting ribbons. Surrounding the spirals are bubbles which themselves form a regular, spaced pattern. The broad glass bases of these so-called Pairpoint weights are intricately engraved and this aspect of the work has been attributed to Carl Banks.

MILLVILLE

Glass-making began at Millville, New Jersey at the beginning of the nineteenth century when a factory for the production of window-glass was established. The Millville glassworks is in operation to this day, though it has undergone a number of changes in name.

RIGHT An amber-ground weight with a boat and lighthouse in opaque white above, attributed to Millville. $3\frac{5}{16}$ in.

LEFT A footed weight with flat motif showing a dog flushing a covey of quail and the motto 'Faithful', made by Millville, attributed to Michael Kane. $3\frac{7}{16}$ in.

BELOW A spatter design above a pebble-ground, both in blue and white, enclosing seven bubbles, made by John St. Clair about 1930. $8\frac{1}{16}$ in.

For much of that period the company was under the direction of the Whitall brothers or Whitall Tatum and Company. Whitall Tatum, best remembered for their tinted glass electric insulators, themselves promoted to the status of collectables in recent years, began producing paperweights as a side-line in the early 1860s. These weights were relatively crude in appearance and seem to have been made as end-of-day ware by the glassworkers. Simple weights depicting a bird perched on the bough of a tree were followed by more elaborate motifs – dogs, horses, scenery and allegorical subjects such as Love and Hope. In the same *genre* is an interesting patriotic weight dating from the Spanish-American War. It features the ill-fated battleship *Maine* sunk in Havana Harbour, and bears the inscription 'Remember the Maine, Feb. 15, 1898'. Other Millville weights dating around the turn of the century featured the emblems of the Freemasons and similar bodies. These weights may be regarded as a distinct form of American folk art and have little artistic pretension.

In sharp contrast to the end-of-day weights are the handsome Millville roses made by outstanding artist-craftsmen such as Ralph Barber, Marcus Kuntz, John Rhulander and Emil Stanger. These are large upright weights with a deep footed base or a balustroid pedestal. Apart from roses Millville's craftsmen also produced tulips and lilies. The most unusual paperweights from this glassworks, however, were those which featured ships, hunting scenes or the American eagle. The decorative motif was a two-dimensional glass picture pressed from a steel matrix and mounted in an upright position. They may be found with plain flattened bases, on footed bases or mounted on pedestals and were often sold as matched pairs for use as mantelpiece ornaments. These picture weights were largely the work of Michael Kane. Paperweight production at Millville seems to have terminated about 1912.

DORFLINGER

Christian Dorflinger (1828–1915), was born in Alsace and learned the craft of glassmaking at St Louis before emigrating to the United States in 1846. Fourteen years later he founded the Green Point Glass Works at Brooklyn, New York but in 1863 he was forced to retire on account of ill health. Two years later, however, he established another company, at White Mills, Pennsylvania. The Dorflinger Glass Works survived its founder by six years but was forced out of business in 1921. Glass paperweights were always a part of Dorflinger's repertoire, ever since the Green Point days when Nicholas Lutz was in his employment. Ralph Barber and Emil Larson, who contributed in no small measure to the output of

BELOW A free-blown pear weight of about 1860 attributed to the New England Glass Co. $2\frac{5}{8}$ in. (COURTESY BERGSTROM ART CENTER)

BELOW A free-form blue-glass bubble weight made by Harvey Littleton in the early 1960s. $3\frac{3}{16}$ in. (COURTESY BERGSTROM ART CENTER)

ABOVE A footed pink water-lily weight surrounded by leaves by Millville. $3\frac{3}{8}$ in. (COURTESY BERGSTROM ART CENTER)

RIGHT A footed yellow rose weight with three leaves by Millville. $3\frac{5}{8}$ in. (COURTESY BERGSTROM ART CENTER)

BELOW LEFT A pink, yellow and white spatter-ground weight with the motto 'Home Sweet Home' attributed to Millville. $3\frac{3}{8}$ in. (COURTESY BERGSTROM ART CENTER)

BELOW A pink and yellow rose weight by Mount Washington, the stem held by a woman's hand. $4\frac{1}{4}$ in. (COURTESY BERGSTROM ART CENTER)

LEFT A pink and blue lily weight on an opaque white ground by Paul Holton of Corning and made in 1941. $3\frac{11}{16}$ in. (COURTESY BERGSTROM ART CENTER)

BELOW A flower spray weight floating above a blue cushion made by Joseph Zimmerman and Gene Baxley in 1967. $3\frac{1}{4}$ in. (COURTESY BERGSTROM ART CENTER)

ABOVE A blue lily weight by Dorflinger with an elongated bubble in the centre. $3\frac{7}{16}$ in. (COURTESY BERGSTROM ART CENTER)

CENTRE An 'under sea' doorstop by Tiffany showing rocks and sea-urchins enclosed in aquamarine glass. $5\frac{5}{16}$ in. (COURTESY BERGSTROM ART CENTER)

ABOVE A pig weight with a green spatter-ground by the Gentile-Funrock Co., about 1947. $3\frac{9}{16}$ in. (COURTESY BERGSTROM ART CENTER)

ABOVE A signed and dated, abstract green-glass weight made by Dominick Labino in 1967. $3\frac{5}{8}$ in. (COURTESY BERGSTROM ART CENTER)

Millville, also worked for Dorflinger at one time or another. Tobias Hagberg and Ernest von Dohln, both of Swedish origin, also produced fine paperweights at the Dorflinger Glass Works. Hagberg 'signed' his paperweights by inserting a small floret in the base which could only be seen when the weight was turned upside down. Von Dohln specialised in large upright weights with blue, red or green four-petalled lily motifs which are quite distinct from the Millville flower weights of the same period.

It is difficult to think in terms of Dorflinger weights as a class, since they were largely the product of craftsmen working in their spare time. The Dorflinger Glass Works was merely a staging post in the careers of Lutz and Larson and even Hagberg's best work in this field was probably done in the late 1920s and 1930s when he was employed by Steuben.

SOMERVILLE

The Union Glass Company of Somerville, Massachusetts is best known for its Kew Blas and other art glass of the 1880s and 1890s, but an astonishing range of paperweights was produced in the early years of this century. One suspects that Nicholas Lutz, who was associated with Somerville between 1895 and his death in 1904, had a hand in this. B. H. Leffingwell, in his account of glassmaking at Somerville, states that Lutz made butterfly, fruit and flower weights at Somerville. Examples of weights containing these subjects, in a style reminiscent of the weights made by Lutz at Sandwich, are known in the characteristically large Somerville format with names and dates which coincide with his Somerville period. Many of the weights produced at this glassworks were inscribed by their makers and intended as Christmas or birthday presents to friends and relatives. For this reason they are frequently dated and inscribed with the name of the recipient.

Two of Lutz's pupils became important glass craftsmen in their own right and both made paperweights which are avidly sought after today. Emil Avinwell was employed by the Union Glass Works until its closure in 1929 and subsequently worked at Pairpoint. He specialised in floral weights with a curious flattened dome, and many of the so-called anniversary weights were his work also. Philip Bunamo also made anniversary weights but his forte was small, high-crowned weights containing upright roses without leaves. Bunamo made strawberry weights, in the Mount Washington idiom, birds' nest weights and curious pig weights containing opaque white piglets or a sulphide sow. A few patriotic weights of First World War vintage, with American and Allied flags, may have been made by Bunamo.

BELOW A spherical butterfly and flower weight by Peter Gentile for the Gentile-Funfrock Co. about 1947. $3\frac{5}{16}$ in.
BOTTOM A black lizard with green spots in a gold and yellow spatter-ground weight, signed 'Harold J. Hacker 1965' on the base. $2\frac{3}{16}$ in.

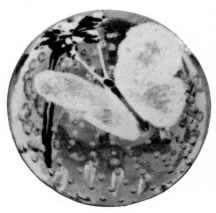

97

STEUBEN

Frederick Carder (1863–1963) learned the craft of glassmaking in his native Brierley, Staffordshire before emigrating to the United States and founding the Steuben Glass Works at Corning, New York in 1903. The setbacks and shortages of the First World War forced Carder out of business, but mercifully his glassworks was rescued by the Corning Glass Company and Carder continued to work there, as art director, until his retirement in 1934. Right down to the end of his very long life, however, he maintained a close interest in the artistic wares for which Steuben is world famous. His own reputation rests mainly on the Cluthra, Aurene and Cintra art glass which was in vogue in the early years of this century, but though he also made some interesting millefiori bowls he is not known to have produced paperweights. As with so many of the other glassworks, paperweights were produced at Steuben as end-of-day ware and were never marketed commercially. Nevertheless a few weights dating from the early 1920s are known with the inscription 'Steuben' on the base. Weights of this type, with five-petalled lilies, were being produced sporadically by Steuben workmen as late as 1942, if not later. Officially Steuben turned away from coloured glass in 1933 and since that time have specialised in clear glass. Consequently the many weights dated after that period and signed 'Steuben' can only be regarded as off-duty products. In the modern Steuben manner, however, some attractive weights have been produced in recent years. Many of these pieces have been experimental in nature and some of them are unique. Paul Schulze has produced a number of abstract geometric pieces and already these are highly prized by discerning collectors. George Thompson has designed a number of *bibelots* which have been released in limited editions with fine engraving by such artists as Tom Vincent, Sidney Wauch and Don Weir.

A bubble mushroom weight of many colours with knob top, made by Jonathan R. Stone at the Indiana Glass Co. in 1967. 3¼ in.

TIFFANY

Louis Comfort Tiffany (1848–1933) is aptly described by his biographer, Robert Koch, as "a rebel in glass", for he did more than any one man to revolutionise the art glass of the late nineteenth century. In 1893 he established the Corona glassworks in Long Island and that year his glassware, shown at the Columbian Exhibition, was hailed as an immediate success. For forty years, until his death, Tiffany produced art glass in the numerous different styles which were appropriate to the period, spanning the years from Art Nouveau to Art Deco. By the beginning of this century Tiffany glass was already considered eminently collectable and, though the company was in production as late as 1936, and its output was vast, such is the magic of the name that even later Tiffany wares are highly prized today, barely forty years after their appearance.

The character of Tiffany glass is quite bewildering in its complexity. Much of the ornamental glass produced during the Art Nouveau period was in the famous 'Tiffany Favrile', characterised by its blue-green shades and penchant for peacock feathers, foliate patterns and underwater frond effects. The range of articles produced in this material was very wide and inevitably included a few paperweights. These Tiffany weights were quite unlike anything else produced at that time and for many years they have been overlooked and despised by collectors of traditional paperweights. They were very much larger and heavier than most other weights and, in this respect, tended to be regarded in the same light as the Kilner doorstop weights referred to in Chapter 9. It is only within the past decade that the significance of Tiffany paperweights has been fully appreciated. Compared to the vases, bowls and lamps the paperweights in Favrile glass were not successful. Technically they were as flawless as anything produced at the Corona glassworks, but it was felt at the time that the ethereal qualities of Favrile were totally unsuited to the solid, massy nature of paperweights – especially paperweights conceived on such a grand scale. Consequently Tiffany produced relatively few of these solid confections. It is only within the past decade, when glass manufacturers have broken away from the millefiori tradition and begun to experiment with new forms and techniques in paperweights, that the aim of the Tiffany weights has been understood and is now being emulated by the new generation of paperweight makers in Britain, Scandinavia and America.

The motifs of the Tiffany weights can only be described as underwater patterns which sometimes resemble jelly-fish or indeterminate marine creatures, and sometimes the waving fronds of seaweed

BELOW A stylised, red and white flower miniature weight on a footed base, made by Charles Kaziun in the early 1960s. $1\frac{7}{16}$ in.

BOTTOM A yellow rose weight on a footed base by Francis Dyer Whittemore in 1965. $2\frac{1}{16}$ in.

LEFT A pressed glass reproduction of Plymouth Rock showing the crack and the date 1620. On the side is a poem and an explanation of the crack, made by the New England Glass Co. $4\frac{1}{8}$ in.

amid rocks. The effect is heightened by the delicate shades of blue and green glass enclosing these motifs. Tiffany weights are often, though not always, signed on the base 'L. C. Tiffany Favrile' with with the serial number of the pattern and a letter indicating the number of the particular weight in that edition.

OTHER OLD AMERICAN WEIGHTS

A large number of American paperweights, manufactured around the turn of the century, exist today but cannot be identified with any degree of certainty. The majority of them are poor in quality and finish and were virtually mass-produced for sale in penny bazaars and at fairgrounds. With the passage of time they have become respectable and, like the seaside picture weights, are now commanding the serious attention of collectors. Among the factories known to have produced such weights in the closing years of the nineteenth century was the B. F. Leach Glass Company of Fowlerton, Indiana. The Fowlerton factory bought mixed broken glass from other factories and used it to produce scrambled weights with banal inscriptions ('My Mother' or 'Home Sweet Home') in mineral ink. Approximately 25,000 of these weights were produced in a two-year period alone and they wholesaled at \$2.50 a dozen. Hollister echoes the sentiments of 'traditional' collectors by dismissing Fowlerton weights contemptuously, looking "as if they were made under a leaky truck crankcase with the sole tool a tire air-hose". Other weights of this era are mercifully shrouded in anonymity.

The discovery of natural gas in the Ohio area in the mid-nineteenth century led to the development of a glass-making industry in that state. Though the products of the Ohio factories were mainly utilitarian, a number of glassworks produced paperweights and other glass novelties. The Zanesville Glass Works, of Zanesville, Ohio produced some excellent free-formed glass birds and animals on a heavy circular base. Flower weights in the Millville manner were made by the Fostoria Glass Company, Ohio between 1880 and 1900. The speciality of this company was a four-petalled lily of red or speckled glass, mounted on an opaque white ground and enclosed in a clear glass dome. Similar flower weights – lilies and trumpet flowers – were manufactured by the Ravenna Glass Company of Ravenna, Ohio about the same time. Ravenna also made flower weights in the form of tall glass cylinders and cubes, and also mounted floral globes on footed pedestals. The Hendrix Works, Findley, Ohio and the Tiffin Glass Company of Tiffin, Ohio are also credited with coloured glass weights and related articles such as door-knobs and inkwells at the end of the nineteenth century. Ohio and neighbouring Indiana are the centres of the modern American

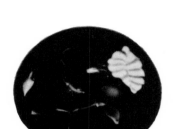

An amethyst-ground weight with a blue and white convolvulus by Charles Kaziun in 1964. 2 in.

A gold-ruby and white rose weight on a footed base, made by John Degenhart about 1950. 2$\frac{11}{16}$ in.

100

paperweight industry, though it is significant that the best work in recent years has been produced by individual artist-craftsmen.

Charles Degenhart (1882–1958) and his brother John (1884–1964), working at Cambridge, Ohio, produced a number of interesting and attractive paperweights in the period from about 1925 to 1950. Many of these are flower weights on heavy footed bases in the Millville tradition, but others featured serpents in coloured glass on a ground of varicoloured glass. John Gentile, working in Morgantown, West Virginia, also made handsome rose weights. The Gentile-Funfrock Glass Company moved to Star City, West Virginia in 1948 and was renamed the Gentile Glass Company. Heavy spherical weights, patented by John G. Funfrock and made by Peter Gentile, show birds and butterflies. trapped in clear glass with a pattern of bubbles. Gertrude Gentile and Frank Hamilton have both made flower weights for this company in recent years. In the 1960s Joseph St Clair made some unusual animal weights at Elwood, Indiana. The animals in white and coloured porcelain were enclosed in clear glass on a coloured glass ground. The St Clair Glass Company acquired crimped sections of caramel coloured glass, made by the Indiana Tumbler and Goblet Company at Greentown at the beginning of this century, and incorporated them in clear glass paperweights manufactured in the early 1960s. Other attractive flower weights have been made in recent years by the Zimmerman Art Glass Company of Corydon, Indiana, by Joseph Zimmerman and Gene Baxley and these weights can be identified by the letter Z impressed on their flattened base. Unusual knob weights, with a protuberance of clear glass rising out of the top of the dome, have been produced by Jonathan Stone at the Indiana Glass Company, Dunkirk, Indiana within the past decade.

MODERN ARTIST-CRAFTSMEN

Pride of place must go to Charles Kaziun of Brockton, Massachusetts for raising modern American paperweights above the level of mediocrity. Largely self-taught, he worked as a glass-blower for a scientific instruments firm before branching out on his own. Under the guidance and inspiration of Emil Larson, Kaziun produced his first rose paperweight in 1942. In the ensuing thirty years Kaziun's output has been enormous and exceedingly diverse. His weights range in size from diminutive buttons to standard three-inch weights, on flat, footed or pedestal bases. Apart from his rose weights Kaziun has perfected other flowers, both flat and upright, in the French classical style – pansy, tulip, crocus, lily, hibiscus, dogwood and morning glory. In addition he has made concentric

An upstanding bouquet weight with one large and five small flowers, made by Frank Hamilton at the Gentile Glass Co. in 1967. 3⅝ in.

A spherical upright flower weight with pink spatter and signed 'Z' on the base, made by Joseph Zimmerman and Gene Baxley in 1967. 3⅜ in.

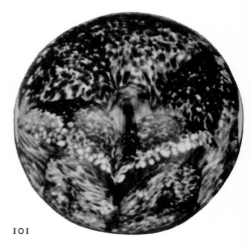

An irregular faceted crystal weight known as 'Star Crystal' made at Steuben, Corning in 1963. 3½ in.

A spray-of-lilies weight in white with blue centres by Gertrude Gentile in 1967. 3³⁄₁₆ in.

millefiori weights on muslin, goldstone and coloured grounds of unusual shade and consistency. He has produced silhouette canes which are distinctive to him – a turtle, a heart, a golden bee, a whale and a seated rabbit. A cane bearing his initial K appears on the bottom of his weights.

Another artist who prefers to work on traditional lines is Francis Dyer Whittemore Jr. of Lansdale, Pennsylvania who has been making footed flower weights in the past ten years. Whittemore, a glassblower with over twenty years experience of the craft, made some excellent miniature figures and scale models before turning to paperweights in the Millville tradition. His little roses are beautifully perfect in every detail. Whittemore weights contain an opaque grey or yellow cane bearing a black W. Ronald Hansen of Mackinaw City, Michigan is another relative newcomer to the paperweight scene. His exuberant flower weights are still in an early stage of their development. The positioning of the motif is usually too low and the facetting too uneven for these weights to rank high at present, but the colouring and composition show immense promise and Hansen's is a name to follow in years to come. Harold Hacker of Bueno Park, California specialises in lizards and snakes on a translucent layer of fine spatter in gold and pale yellow glass simulating sand. These weights are inscribed 'Harold J. Hacker' with the date on the base. Hacker has also produced a number of flower weights, with preference for the poinsettia. Hacker's weights date from 1965.

Breaking away from traditional patterns and techniques are Dominik Labino, Harvey Littleton and Adolph Mocho. Labino of Grand Rapids, Ohio makes paperweights in tinted glass, shades of green and blue, containing air pockets in abstract designs. These weights are inscribed 'Labino' and the date on the underside. Harvey K. Littleton, of Verona, Wisconsin, has been making interesting free-form paperweights in coloured glass since the early 1960s. His large mushroom-shaped weights achieve their effect by trapping one or more large air bubbles and have dark canes which extend vertically all the way from the base to the crown. These tall asymmetrical weights derive inspiration from the oriental pottery which Littleton studied and emulated in the early part of his career. Adolph Mocho works at the Vineland glassworks in New Jersey where, at an earlier date, Emil Larson was also employed. Mocho's weights are traditional in profile but contain unusual butterfly motifs and grounds in spatters of different colours. These weights are signed 'A. Mocho' on a partially frosted base.

102

Twelve

European Paperweights

The brilliance of the French, Bohemian and Venetian paperweights of the classic period overshadowed paperweight production everywhere else and it is only in recent years that collectors have turned their attention to the products of other countries. At the same time the art of the paperweight has been revived in countries where it was long defunct, or has spread to countries which never made them in the classic period. Purely for the sake of convenience these predominantly modern examples of paperweight manufacture are grouped together in this chapter.

BELGIAN PAPERWEIGHTS

Glass paperweights are known to have been made at half a dozen factories in Belgium in the nineteenth century. The Bougard glassworks at Jumet, near Charleroi, made curious abstract flower weights about 1850, while the *Verreries Nationales*, situated in the same town, produced crude flower weights about 1880. Paperweights of relatively poor quality were manufactured at the glassworks in the Brussels and Namur districts. Sulphide paperweights, usually with a religious motif, were made at Chenee, near Liège, at the end of the nineteenth century.

The bulk of Belgian paperweight production was carried out at the Val St Lambert factory, the largest of the nineteenth century Belgian glasshouses. The company was founded in 1825 at Seraing near Liège by Francois Kemlin and Auguste LeLievre who were originally associated with d'Artigues in the Voneche glassworks. In 1825 they split up, Kemlin and LeLievre going to Val St Lambert and d'Artigues to Baccarat. When Baccarat began making millefiori paperweights the Val St Lambert company agreed not to compete in this field. This plausible explanation is advanced by Evelyn Campbell Cloak in *Glass Paperweights* to account for the paucity of Val St Lambert weights and the relatively limited number of different millefiori canes which that factory used. Too little is known, however, about the production of paperweights at Val St Lambert for this theory to be tested. The few Val St Lambert weights which have been recorded are comparable in quality to those of Baccarat and why production should have been so limited remains a mystery. Because they were unconsidered until recently, it may well be that Val St Lambert weights are still lying around in Belgian attics and cupboards awaiting rediscovery and the reappraisal which is long overdue.

Val St Lambert favoured an upright rectangular profile for overlay weights, enclosing a globular motif. Ordinary weights had a rounder profile and were usually heavily facetted. The glass was very light and usually had a slightly yellowish cast. The majority of recorded specimens have coloured or muslin grounds with a single cane in the centre. Val St Lambert also made spaced, patterned and concentric millefiori weights but these are of the greatest rarity. A few flower weights featuring pansies and indeterminate species are attributed to this company. Several Val St Lambert weights contain inscriptions which seem to suggest that they were intended as presentation pieces. Occasional weights with oval printies and elaborate star-cutting were being produced at Val St Lambert as late as the 1920s.

So far as the writer is aware no paperweights are being made in Belgium at the present time, though some partially successful attempts in this field have been made in neighbouring Holland. Modern Dutch paperweights are currently exploring new profiles in coloured glass with spatters of opaque colour and long elliptical bubbles in abstract patterns.

SCANDINAVIAN PAPERWEIGHTS

The most outstanding contributions to modern glass have been made by the Swedish factories and the paperweight has also benefited to a large extent from the imagination and technical virtuosity of the Swedish designers and craftsmen. Very little is known of the antecedents of paperweight production in Scandinavia. A few sulphides are recorded from the late nineteenth century, but though they have Danish or Swedish motifs they may have been produced in France for export to Scandinavia. The Bergstrom Art Center has a Danish paperweight, thought to have been produced sometime between 1880 and 1920. This very large and heavy weight

Owl weight by Erik Hoglund of Boda, Sweden.

Hoglund's owl weight from another angle.

is of clear colourless glass and encloses near the top of the crown a layer of coarse, varicoloured pebble glass, through which five elongated bubbles extend downwards to a second layer of pebble ground. The entire motif floats about an inch above the flat base of the weight. The same museum has a Swedish weight dating from the early part of this century. The pale creamy glass encloses two layers of coarse spatter glass, predominantly orange, into which a large central bubble and four smaller elongated bubbles extend downwards. It is not known which factories were responsible for these Danish and Swedish weights.

Modern Swedish paperweights date from the early 1960s and are as revolutionary in style as they were sudden and dramatic in appearance. Among the first in the field was the Orrefors glassworks whose clear glass weights have an austere, geometric simplicity. They consist of rectangles and squares enclosing clear glass hearts, crosses and other symbols and they are the work of Gunnar Cyren and Ingeborg Lundin.

Orrefors has been overtaken by the Kosta glassworks which now produces the widest range of paperweights in many different forms and using diverse techniques. Globular weights in clear crystal glass have the traditional profile, but contain patterns of fine bubbles which are thoroughly modern in concept. In 1964 Mona Morales-Schildt began making cylindrical paperweights at Kosta. These *bibelots* as she calls them achieve their startling effect by the clever use of layers of glass of different colours, so that a third colour is created where the two overlap. Other weights made by her in recent years, include layered cylinders of different colours, exposed by cutting concave windows in the manner of the old overlay weights. Some of these weights are cubes and polygons as well as cylinders and their overall effect is most unusual.

Vicke Lindstrand of Kosta specialises in engraved and etched glass weights. Her 'iceberg' weights consist of rough chunks of greenish glass engraved from beneath or behind with scenery, animals or birds. The motif is viewed through the rough texture of the glass and the resulting effect is very pleasing. In the early 1960s Miss Lindstrand produced rectangles, triangles and hexagons of clear, colourless glass with facets cut on the sides and corners, and portraits of famous people, such as Dag Hammarskjold, John F. Kennedy, Alexander Graham Bell and Albert Schweitzer engraved on the underside. These portrait weights are signed and bear the number of the weight in each limited edition.

Strömbergshyttan began with curious green algae set in clear crystal and have now progressed to glass toadstools. Spatters of different colours appear under the clear, irregularly-shaped top and

Seal weight in clear, colourless glass by Hadeland of Norway.

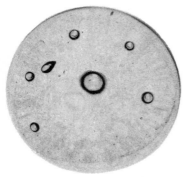

the whole is mounted on a globular base. The name of the company appears in cursive script incised on the flat base of the globe. The F. M. Konstglas company of Ronneby has produced excellent abstract weights with streaks of pink opaque glass over black, resembling a sea-urchin. Reijmyre has specialised in animal and bird forms in various coloured glass. Paperweights in the shape of animals and birds are to be found in Norway, the product of anonymous glassworks, but this medium has been developed to an artistic peak in Finland, especially by Kaj Franck of the Wartsila-Nuutajärvi glasshouse. He received his artistic training in ceramics, but since 1959 has concentrated on coloured glass with a regular aerated pattern and has produced some outstanding bird figures in this medium.

OTHER COUNTRIES

There was a flourishing industry in Germany, up to the time of the First World War, in large coloured marbles, up to $7\frac{1}{2}$ inches in diameter, containing threads of opaque or clear coloured glass and occasionally with a fine latticinio spiral running through the centre. It seems logical that similar objects, with a flattened base, should have been produced as paperweights, and yet they seem conspicuous by their absence. At the same time, from about 1880 to 1914, a few small paperweights with a millefiori base were made in Germany for export to Britain and America. The canes were coarse and garishly coloured and the glass dome was full of minute bubbles and impurities. Since the Second World War globular weights have been made in West Germany in clear glass with a pale yellowish tinge, and containing floral patterns made of small chips of coloured glass.

Small, ovoid weights in colourless or bluish glass with spaced pinprick bubbles near the surface were made in Spain in the years before the Civil War. It is sad to reflect that a country which was renowned for its glass in the Middle Ages when the Moorish influence was at its height, should have been reduced to pathetic baubles of this sort.

Paperweights of traditional shape are now being made at Mdina in Malta, but differ from anything which has gone before in their content. A hemisphere of native Maltese stone is encapsulated in clear glass and the result is a pleasing paperweight in yellow or brown or deep green streaked with yellow. These Maltese weights are quite inexpensive and are designed as tourist souvenirs of the island, but they have the merit of originality and it is significant that they are now turning up in the better sort of china and crystal shop

in Britain.

Thirteen

Asian Paperweights

It is a sad commentary on the degeneration of a nation that it should be reduced to copying the arts and crafts of others and failing lamentably in the process. That a race so talented and inventive as the Chinese should have been reduced to making tawdry imitations of old French and American paperweights seems somehow to symbolise the state of that country in the inter-war years. Shortly after the First World War, when the market in classic weights began to harden, some astute American *entrepreneurs* despatched a consignment of genuine weights to Shanghai and Canton, whence they found their way into the hands of skilful imitators. From a handful of originals the Chinese were able to produce thousands of imitations which flooded the American and European markets. One of the benefits of the Communist takeover in the immediate post-war years was that this doubtful trade was brought to a halt.

Fake Chinese weights do not deceive anyone with a modicum of knowledge about the genuine article, or a critical eye in his or her head. Primarily the pre-war Chinese weights were encased in glass of the poorest quality, a general fuzziness and yellowish cast being combined with minute bubbles and impurities. The Chinese attempted to duplicate the intricate millefiori canes of Baccarat and Cambridge, but never mastered the technique. The colours of the rods tended to be the most violent of primaries with a curious predilection for a jaundiced yellow floret with a pillar-box red centre. There is a looseness about these millefiori florets, as though the components had fragmented on impact. The spirals and threads of the latticinio lacked opacity and the set-up of the canes was irregular. There was a comical tendency to confuse the decoration of Baccarat with the profile of Millville or the faceting of New England. Now and again a pleasing effect would be achieved, almost accidentally, but the majority of the pre-war Chinese weights were poor, insipid copies of the classic weights. There is still a distressing amount of these forgeries about, though little experience is required to detect them.

After a decent interval Chinese paperweights have again made their appearance on the market and although they cling to the traditional millefiori pattern they are openly sold for what they are – cheap Chinese weights. There is a noticeable improvement in the encasing glass, though that yellowish cast is still present, and the appearance of the canes has been smartened up considerably. It has to be conceded that many modern Chinese weights show evidence

Chinese miniature millefiori carpet-ground weight with red, yellow, white and blue canes.

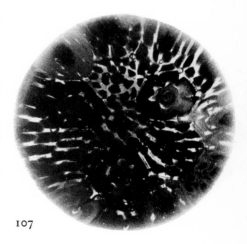

of skill and fine workmanship and, with time, these inscrutable baubles, with their cryptic 'Made in China' paper labels pasted to the base, may rival modern European millefiori weights. But this is being optimistic. Perhaps the Chinese will eventually settle for their own distinctive brand of millefiori and give up the unequal struggle to emulate St Louis and Whitefriars.

Apart from the millefiori weights the Chinese have produced a wide variety of flower weights (more or less imitating the Millville rose or the Baccarat pansy), sulphides of animals, birds, frogs and insects, some quite attractive sailing ships and nautical scenes, and a few landscape weights in which the motif is painted on an opaque base in the oriental manner. It was long fashionable to decry *all* Chinese paperweights and condemn them out of hand as an abomination; but the more discerning or open-minded collectors are now conceding that some Chinese weights are worthy of a place in their collections.

JAPANESE PAPERWEIGHTS

Some of the weights classified as pre-war Chinese may, in fact, have been produced in Japan, but the manufacture of paperweights in Japan today is quite distinctive. Cheap and nasty glass weights began to find their way on to Western markets from Japan in the late 1950s and undoubtedly deserved Hollister's scathing condemnation of them. He has dismissed them curtly, grouping the small lily weights and "macerated slices of cane floating aimlessly in clear glass" with the plastic snow-storm weights which Japan (and now Hong Kong) produce for the delectation of small children.

But the pattern of Japanese paperweights, like everything else produced in Japan, has changed radically in recent years. The Japanese are no longer content to copy the West but, having taken hold of an object, they have modified it or developed it along distinctive lines. Thus the better Japanese weights of the past decade deserve serious attention. Among the more interesting of these contemporary weights are those in moulded glass of the ribbed-melon pattern in colourless glass enclosing an elliptical sphere of deep blue or ruby glass. The Japanese have also produced some passable bullet-shaped weights enclosing three dimensional groups

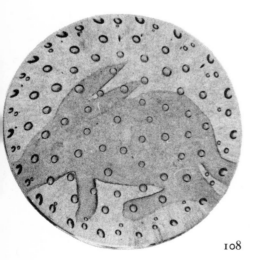

ABOVE LEFT Tiny upright weight with green, pink and red flowers on a scrambled millefiori base. Chinese.

LEFT Miniature Chinese weight in clear glass with overall bubble pattern and a rabbit etched on the base.

Upright Indian weight
containing 3 flowers in
a multi-coloured
spatter.

of lilies and morning glory. One has only to remember the extraordinary facility of the Japanese in the production of industrial glassware and lenses to appreciate that here is a force to be reckoned with. The future looks very promising for Japanese paperweights, particularly if traditional Japanese art forms were explored and developed.

INDIA

In recent years high-crowned paperweights 'hand blown in India', according to the red and gold label affixed to their base, have come on to the market. These weights are inexpensive, are encased in reasonably clear glass and have wisely avoided the pitfalls of the prewar Chinese weights by leaving millefiori patterns alone and concentrating on distinctive modes of decoration. Indian paperweights favour an upright floral motif, with three or four lilies whose petals are composed vaguely of an opaque coloured spatter. Here again one would hope that the glassworkers of India would tap the rich vein of indigenous art forms for future inspiration, rather than produce an uneasy compromise with occidental motifs.

Bibliography

Bedford, John *Paperweights*, Cassells London (1968)

Bergstrom, Evangeline H. *Old Glass Paperweights*, Crown Pub. New York (1947), Faber (1948)

Bergstrom Paperweight Symposium *Booklet of the Symposium*, Neenah, Wisconsin (1967)

Bozek, Michael *Price Guide Handbook of Glass Paperweights*, Hollywood (1961)

Cloak, Evelyn Campbell *Glass Paperweights*, Studio Vista London (1969)

Elville, E. M. *Paperweights and Other Glass Curiosities*, Country Life London (1954)

Hollister, Paul Jr *The Encyclopedia of Glass Paperweights*, C. N. Potter New York (1969)

Honey, W. B. *English Glass*, Collins London (1946)

Imbert, Roger and Amic, Yolande *Les Presse-Papiers Français*, Rataet Industrie Paris (1948)

Jokelson, Paul *Antique French Paperweights*, New York (1955)
One Hundred of the Most Important Paperweights, New York (1966)
Sulphides, Nelson New York (1968)

Koch, Robert *Louis C. Tiffany: Rebel in Glass*, Crown Pub. New York (1964)

McCawley, Patricia K. *Antique Glass Paperweights from France*, Spink & Son London (1968)

Mackay, James A. *Antiques of the Future*, Studio Vista London (1970)

McKearin, George S. and Helen *American Glass*, Crown Pub. New York (1941), Batsford (1947)

Manheim, Frank J. *A Garland of Weights*, Farrar Strans New York (1967)

Melvin, Jean Sutherland *American Glass Paperweights and their Makers*, Nelson New York (1967)

Pellatt, Apsley *Curiosities of Glass Making*, David Bogue London (1849)

Smith, Francis Edgar *American Glass Paperweights*, Wollaston, Massachusetts (1939)

Watkins, Lura W. *Cambridge Glass 1818–1888*, Marshall Jones Boston (1930)

Informative articles on various aspects of paperweights and their production have appeared in the following periodicals at various times. Readers would be advised to consult the indices of these magazines for details:

The American Antiques Collector, American Collector, Antiques, The Antiques Journal, Collectors Guide, Hobbies and *Spinning Wheel*.

The Paperweight Collectors' Association publishes a regular bulletin. For details of membership and the bulletin write to Paul Jokelson, 47 Windsor Road, Scarsdale, New York.

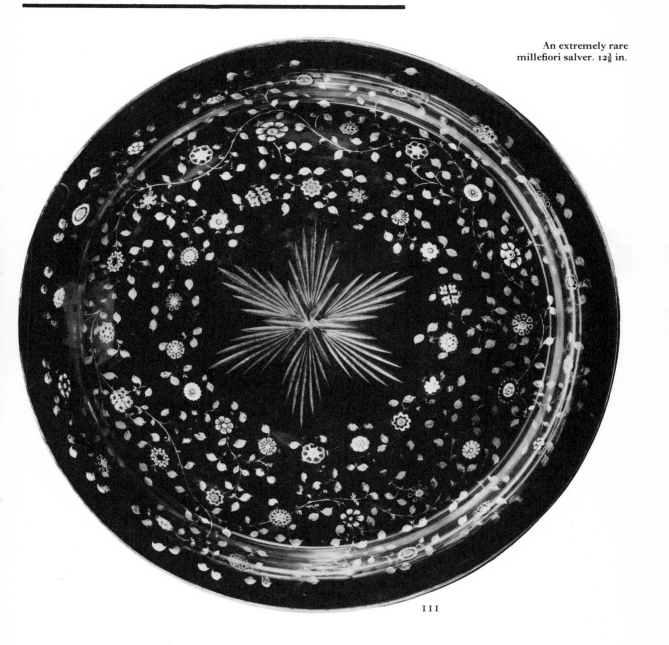

An extremely rare millefiori salver. 12⅜ in.

Index